Echoes of Faith

Devotions on the Psalms We Sing

Evelyn Laycock

Abingdon Press
Nashville

To

William A. (Bill) Laycock, Jr.,

a son who put a psalm of praise

in his mother's heart

ECHOES OF FAITH
DEVOTIONS ON THE PSALMS WE SING

Copyright © 2003 by Abingdon Press

This book is printed on acid-free, recycled paper.

ISBN 0-687-04815-X

03 04 05 06 07 08 09 10 11 12 — 10 9 8 7 6 5 4 3 2 1

MANUFACTURED IN THE UNITED STATES OF AMERICA

Contents

1. Introduction 5

2. The Two Roads of Life 9
   Psalm 1 15
   "I Shall Not Be Moved" 15

3. A Universal Question: Who Am I? 16
   Psalm 8 22
   "Joyful, Joyful, We Adore Thee" 22

4. The Lord Is My Shepherd 23
   Psalm 23 34
   "The Lord's My Shepherd, I'll Not Want" 34

5. Can You Hear Me, Lord? 35
   Psalm 51 40
   "O For a Heart to Praise My God" 41

6. An Attitude of Gratitude 43
   Psalm 103 50
   "Praise, My Soul, the King of Heaven" 51

7. The Palm Sunday Journey 52
   Psalm 118 57
   "This Is the Day the Lord Hath Made" 58

8. Psalms from the Cross 59
   Psalm 22 66
   "O Sacred Head, Now Wounded" 67

9. The Other Bookend 68
   Psalm 150 69
   "Praise to the Lord, the Almighty" 70

Chapter 1

Introduction

The book of Psalms is a favorite of many, for its pages are filled with everyday issues that affect all of us: hope/despair; joy/pain; worship/abandonment; love/hate; prayer/isolation; praise/silence; music/cacophony.

For example, have you ever experienced a time in your life when you asked the provocative question, "In this great universe where do I fit in God's plan?" A psalmist, too, had that struggle. "When I look at your heavens, the work of your fingers, the moon and the stars that you have established; what are human beings that you are mindful of them, mortals that you care for them?" (Ps. 8:3-4).

Have you ever felt abandoned by God, left completely alone only to see your enemies being elevated, praised, and honored? Listen to the psalmist who felt those same emotions. "How long, O LORD? Will you forget me forever? How long will you hide your face from me? How long must I bear pain in my soul, and have sorrow in my heart all day long? How long shall my enemy be exalted over me?" (Ps. 13:1, 2).

Do you recall a time when you felt especially vulnerable or threatened? Perhaps you knew such uncertainty on September 11, 2001, and during the difficult months that followed that terrible day. This psalmist knew such a day when he cried out: "Guard me as the apple of the eye; hide me in the shadow of your wings, from the wicked who despoil me, my deadly enemies who surround me" (Ps. 17:8-9).

Have you experienced the heaviness of guilt over sin in your life? That was the experience of the writer of Psalm 51, generally acknowledged to be King David, when he felt the full impact of the sin in his life. "Create in me a clean heart, O God, and put a new and right spirit within me. Do not cast me away from your presence, and do not take your holy spirit from me. Restore to me the joy of your salvation, and sustain in me a willing spirit" (Ps. 51:10-12).

Do you remember the gratitude you felt when God delivered you from sin or other obstacles that the evil one placed in your path? The psalmist expresses thanksgiving for God's deliverance: "I love you, O LORD, my strength. The LORD is my rock, my fortress, and my deliverer, my God, my rock in whom I take refuge, my shield, and the horn of my salvation, my stronghold. I call upon the LORD, who is worthy to be praised, so shall I be saved from my enemies" (Ps. 18:1-3).

Are there times when your whole being yearns for more and more of God's presence and power? The psalmist might have expressed your deep feelings in these words: "As a deer longs for flowing streams, so my soul longs for you, O God. My soul thirsts for God, for the living God" (Ps. 42:1-2b).

In the hectic schedule of life have you experienced the overwhelming absence of having a quiet center within, feeling only chaos? The writer of Psalm 46 gives a great pathway to inner serenity. "Be still, and know that I am God!" (Ps. 46:10a).

The psalmist shared your emotions at being overwhelmed with the goodness and greatness of God as words of praise and thanksgiving flowed from deep within him as from a fountain of living water. "Praise the LORD, all you nations! Extol him, all you peoples! For great is his steadfast love toward us, and the faithfulness of the LORD endures forever. Praise the LORD!" (Ps. 117).

The book of Psalms is as relevant to life in the twenty-first century as the evening news, tomorrow's newspaper, and information from the Internet. Because of the universal message about the "stuff" out of which life is made—hunger for God, disappointment with what life has brought, the yearning to praise God, the depths of rejection, the beauty of nature, the dark night of the soul, the faithfulness of God, and the joy of worshiping—the Psalms became the first hymnbook of the Temple. Are not these the feelings, yearnings, and concerns of modern life? Technology changes the mechanisms of our lives but our yearning for God, our despair over our sin, our need for God's protection, our joy in God's presence—all are timeless and free of technological evolution. From Adam and Eve to the time when all of humankind are face-to-face with God, these never change. At any moment one can find a psalm that speaks to a specific need and gives language for deep feelings or yearnings to be expressed. Often, as I am reading a psalm, I know that it is "my psalm" for it gives expression to my soul. It then becomes my prayer. This universal appeal is evident because the book of Psalms is both humanity's words to God and God's words to humanity. It reflects a dynamic dialogue between God and persons. As such, salvation becomes a way of being in the everydayness of life—an intimate relationship with God that calls forth singing!

One of the unique features of the Psalms is that many contain words that one could not say in the Temple—language that would be considered blasphemy. For example, one could not say, "My God, my God, why have you forsaken me?" However, the question was burning in the soul and would not go away. How could one express such an unorthodox question to God? You could sing it! So, the Psalms found their way into Hebrew worship as hymns and gave the hearts of the worshipers a freedom of expression to God.

Another unique aspect of the book of Psalms is that many of the Psalms portray persons talking to God; most of the Holy Bible reveals God talking to persons. In the books written by the prophets there is the recurring phrase "Thus says the LORD," indicating that God is speaking to people. Many of the Psalms are recordings of God's dialogue with persons as they express heartfelt questions and listen for God's response. Look at the boldness of their questions:

- "Why, O LORD, do you stand far off? Why do you hide yourself in times of trouble?" (Ps. 10:1)
- "How long, O LORD? Will you be angry forever? Will your jealous wrath burn like fire?" (Ps. 79:5)
- "Incline your ear, O LORD, and answer me, for I am poor and needy." (Ps. 86:1)
- "O LORD, you God of vengeance, you God of vengeance, shine forth!" (Ps. 94:1)

Such honest expressions show a deep faith in God as One who hears and responds.

Many in the United States can relate to songs that were born out of the deep hurts of slavery. Slaves talked with God through music in order to endure the brutalities of daily life in slavery. Spirituals, such as "Nobody Knows the Trouble I've Seen" and "Go Down, Moses" tell of this hard reality and express the cry for Jesus to be with them. The words of the following hymn record the cry of the heart for intimacy with Jesus.

1. I want Jesus to walk with me.
I want Jesus to walk with me.
All along my pilgrim journey,
Lord, I want Jesus to walk with me.

2. In my trials, Lord, walk with me.
In my trials, Lord, walk with me.
When my heart is almost breaking,
Lord, I want Jesus to walk with me.

3. When I'm troubled, Lord, walk with me. *Hymnnal P.52.*
   When I'm troubled, Lord, walk with me.
   When my head is bowed in sorrow,
   Lord, I want Jesus to walk with me.[1]

Do you hear a similar theme from the Hebrew writer who penned these words?

> As a deer longs for flowing streams,
>   so my soul longs for you, O God.
> My soul thirsts for God,
>   for the living God. (Ps. 42:1-2a)

In our Judeo-Christian faith the strong appeal of the book of Psalms cannot be questioned. Written by many hands, through many years, by persons in a variety of situations, the Psalms articulate God's will for humankind—justice, righteousness, and peace established among all peoples and all nations. And God seeks a relationship with all persons in order that life will have meaning, purpose, and joy.

The teachings we glean from the Psalms cannot be completely gathered in an earthly lifetime. As we journey together through these selected ancient writings certain themes will be used, themes that are relevant concerns and issues in the twenty-first century.

We will let these ancient writings speak and serve as a guide, both to the present and the future. The pages of the book of Psalms allow us to lift up the rooftop of ancient history in order to observe, study, reflect, listen, and learn. In so doing we go back to the future. May it be an exciting, challenging, and meaningful journey.

As we begin our meditations may we pray with the psalmist:

> For God alone my soul waits in silence;
>   from him comes my salvation.
> He alone is my rock and my salvation,
>   my fortress; I shall never be shaken. (Ps. 62:1-2)

Chapter 2

The Two Roads of Life

The LORD watches over the way of the righteous,
but the way of the wicked will perish.

Psalm 1:6

Psalms 1 and 150 are called "bookends," for they are the first and last writings in the book of Psalms. Psalm 1 is the preface or introduction to the Psalter; Psalm 150 is the concluding hymn of praise. These two psalms also have the distinction of being a summary of all the pages in between, similar to a *Reader's Digest* version of the Psalms. In these two psalms we find the common theological threads that are highly visible throughout the entire book: praise, happiness, wickedness, prosperity, God's gracious gifts, and the absence of pleasure for the wicked. These are commonly used expressions in the English language but, to be faithful to the texts of Scripture, we must first look at them through the eyes of the authors and the Middle Eastern culture in which they lived.

We understand the need to view the Psalms from this perspective when we realize how many English words have changed their meaning in the recent past. For example, a "mouse" used to be thought of as a little creature with four feet that scared some people; now, a mouse is held in one's hand in order to operate the computer. "Cool" used to only refer to temperature; now it also means great/accepted/OK. We mow grass; now the word "grass" also means a hallucinogenic drug. Words have changed both in our culture and in Middle Eastern culture. A word translated literally from Middle Eastern languages may have a totally different meaning to us. That is why contextual Bible study is so necessary, freeing, and exciting.

An example of this is found in Psalm 1. The psalm opens with the word *blessed*, which is often translated "happy." If we would ask a Middle Eastern person the meaning of *blessed* we would hear with great enthusiasm that it means "Oh, the sheer joy!" Happiness comes from external circumstances, when life is going well and no major problems are being encountered—happiness is only skin deep. Joy is different—joy is an inward state of being that is present regardless of the outward circumstances. Joy goes to the marrow of our bones, the center of our being. Joy comes from a right relationship with God,

9

with self, and with others. In the book *Maria* by the Georgia author Eugenia Price, the question is asked, "What is joy?"[2] The profound response is "Joy might be God—in the marrow of our bones."

The apostle Paul would agree with this definition, and he reminded us that "We know that all things work together for good for those who love God, who are called according to his purpose" (Rom. 8:28). This allows us to have joy in all circumstances because we know that every situation will ultimately be for our best interest and for the glory of God, as long as we are in right relationship with God. God gives a bone marrow transplant of joy. The psalmist states that such joy is found in persons who (1) do not follow the advice of the wicked; (2) do not adopt the lifestyle of sinners; and (3) do not sit in the seat of scoffers. (Middle Eastern persons believe that to mock God is the root cause of sin.)

Resting Place

REFLECTIONS

Recall a time in your life when you felt your world had caved in on you. Then, through your steadfast commitment to God in the situation, great joy and new life grew out of it.

PRAYER

"I will praise you, O Lord, with all my heart; I will tell of all your wonders. I will be glad and rejoice in you; I will sing praise to your name, O Most High." Amen. (Ps. 9:1-2 NIV)

We have defined the word *joy*, now we need to see the meaning of the word *sin* or *sinners* as understood by the psalmist. This is necessary because often sin is seen as not obeying a set of rules given by the church, our parents, or our culture. I can remember some of those rules, which stated that a Christian doesn't smoke, dance, curse, play cards, drink alcohol, or participate in a multitude of additional activities considered "do nots." One can abstain from all of these and still have evil in the heart. These are external characteristics only and are not a barometer of a person's relationship with Christ. Matthew is describing such a condition when he says, "You blind Pharisee! First clean the inside of the cup, so that the outside also may become clean" (Matt. 23:26).

I understand the use of the word *cup* in Matthew's illustration. I am often away from the office on teaching assignments, and if I do not clean my coffee cup before leaving the office, when I return the stale coffee contains some kind of biological hazard floating on top. I am afraid to ask what it is. When I see the inside of the cup in this condition, the words of Matthew remind me to ask, "Do I focus on looking like a Christian rather than being like Christ? Am I open to God's inner cleansing of my mind, body, soul, and relationships?" Answering these questions is always a challenge, and a line from the Psalms soon becomes my prayer: "Create in me a clean heart, O God, and put a new and right spirit within me" (Ps. 51:10).

In both the Old and New Testaments the definition of sin is "not being what we are created to be." Sin is not an outward act or a series of acts, sin is considered to be the inner condition that allows the act(s) to be possible. Being created in God's image means that each day persons are to be centered in God's will and become channels of God's justice, righteousness, and mercy in the everydayness of life. This is why the psalmist can boldly state that persons who seek to be God-centered cannot follow the advice of the wicked or adopt their way of life or sit with those who scoff God. This theme weaves its way through the entire book of Psalms as well as through all the pages of the Bible.

Resting Place

REFLECTIONS
- Is there a parallel between my daily life and my beliefs?
- Am I willing to surrender what I must for God to create in me a clean heart?
- From the perspective of sin defined as "not being what you are created to be," read the front page of today's newspaper. As you read ask, "How would this article be different if each of the persons mentioned were living in the potential of his or her creation?"

PRAYER
Cleansing God, I bring myself to you for a thorough washing. Make me clean in soul, mind, body, and relationships, so that I can be a channel of your love, truth, grace, and joy this day. Amen.

Part 2

The psalmist continues by giving a positive portrayal of those who are experiencing God's joy. "Their delight is in the law of the LORD and on his law they meditate day and night" (Ps. 1:2). Some have taken this to be legalistic code but this is not in keeping with the language of the text. The Hebrew word used for law fundamentally means "instruction." Joy-filled persons delight in constant openness to God, enjoying fellowship and new learning opportunities. This is radically different from a set of legalistic codes. This God-centered relationship is the focus of all of life. It is the lighthouse that directs the person to God's will in any and all areas.

In Nathaniel Hawthorne's writings, there is a delightful story called "The Great Stone Face." The central character is a boy named Ernest who lives in a small village in the valley. High on the mountain above the village is an outcropping of rocks that forms the face of a noble, pleasant, kind man. This is called the Great Stone Face. Ernest spends many hours meditating on this face, even talking to it at times. Ernest developed a close bond with the face.

An old legend circulating in the valley stated that at some future day a boy child will be born who is destined to become the greatest and noblest person of his time. His countenance in manhood should bear resemblance to the Great Stone Face. Ernest yearns to see this person in his lifetime but, just as in previous years, the prophecy is not fulfilled. Ernest grows old and his hopes begin to fade.

One evening as Ernest is in the village talking with his many friends, a poet in the midst shouts, "Behold! Behold! Ernest is himself the likeness of the Great Stone Face!" Ernest, through the years of looking at and admiring the Great Stone Face had come to embody those very characteristics that he loved and found present in the face. [3]

It is a fact of life that we become like that on which we meditate. Therefore, those who are joy-filled have a constant openness to God's teaching.

Resting Place

REFLECTIONS

Think about the last twenty-four hours. Who or what was the center of your meditation?

PRAYER

On today's journey, O God, keep me focused on being the visible expression of your Kingdom on earth as it is in heaven. Amen.

Part 3

The psalmist continues to describe joy-filled persons by using the simile of trees. "They are like trees planted by streams of water, which yield their fruit in its season, and their leaves do not wither. In all that they do they prosper" (Ps. 1:3). What beautiful imagery —persons who are continually open for God's instruction, guidance, and power are rooted by life-giving streams that nourish continuously, never lacking the necessities for growth and productivity. This results from being deeply rooted in ground that can withstand drought. To entrust one's life to God is to always have the resources necessary to sustain life regardless of the external circumstances. This is a promise from God.

We hear the promise "In all that they do they prosper." Most of us immediately connect prosperity to material things, such as money, houses, cars, jewelry, and clothes. Is this what the psalmist meant? I think not. The psalmist understood prosperity as being connected to the source of life—God. The joy-filled person knows God and has the absolute assurance of being in a life-giving relationship that will survive any experience that life may bring.

While teaching in Israel I came upon a Palestinian Christian friend I had known and loved for many years. His life has been very difficult but he never complains. He radiates hope, love, and "thanks-living." I asked Zakki, "What would be prosperity for you?" He thought for a short time and then said, "I am prosperous. God is my partner in life. My wife and children love me. What more could I want?" Just like the psalmist, Zakki knows the meaning of true prosperity.

Resting Place

REFLECTIONS
What would be prosperity for you?

PRAYER
O God of Love, forgive me for seeing prosperity through the eyes of my culture instead of always seeking first your Kingdom, where prosperity is truly experienced. Amen.

Part 4

We move now to additional references in the psalm about the wicked. An emphatic contrast is given concerning the wicked and the righteous:

- Righteous persons are like trees planted by streams of water; the wicked are like chaff that the wind blows away.
- The righteous have deep roots that are nourished by the waters; the wicked have no roots but are blown at the discretion of the wind.
- The righteous bear fruit; the wicked are fruitless with no connection to the source of life.
- The righteous prosper; the wicked are in a state of instability and uselessness.

We are presented with the sharpest contrast between the "way of the righteous" and the "way of the wicked." The righteous are those who are rooted in God, are constantly open to God's teaching, and are always in a right relationship with God. They experience joy. On the other hand, the wicked choose not to be related to God, make their own decisions, and take pride in being autonomous. Because of this choice they will perish. These two ways to live an earthly life and their results are frequent themes in the book of Psalms, as well as in the entire Bible.

My husband Bill and I enjoy reading license plates on cars and wondering about the story behind what is on the plate. Recently as we were driving on I-40 toward Nashville, a car passed us with a license plate displaying the capital letters, I CHOOSE. I couldn't help wondering, "Did the driver choose God or choose to be autonomous?" The answer will determine if his life is joy-filled or in a state of instability and desolation.

Resting Place

REFLECTIONS FOR JOURNALING
- Select a person you believe to be a "tree planted by the streams of water." What fruits are in evidence in his or her life?
- Consider the meaning of the phrase "the way of the wicked will perish." Explain how it is an experience in the present. Explain how it is also future related.
- What does it mean to you when you read that the righteous meditate on God's law day and night?

PRAYER
Help me, O God, to discern your will in all things. May my constant prayer be "not my will, but thy will be done in my life today." Amen.

Psalm 1

Happy are those who do not follow
    the advice of the wicked,
  or take the path that sinners tread,
    or sit in the seat of scoffers;
but their delight is in the law of the LORD,
    and on his law they meditate day and night.
They are like trees
    planted by streams of water,
which yield their fruit in its season,
    and their leaves do not wither.
In all that they do, they prosper.
The wicked are not so,
    but are like chaff that the wind
    drives away.
Therefore the wicked will not
    stand in the judgment,
nor sinners in the
    congregation of the righteous;
for the LORD watches over the
    way of the righteous,
but the way of the wicked will perish.

new Revised Standard Version

I Shall Not Be Moved
Traditional African American Spiritual

1. I shall not, I shall not be moved.
I shall not, I shall not be moved,
just like a tree that's planted by the water
I shall not be moved.

2. Jesus is my captain, I shall not be moved.
Jesus is my captain, I shall not be moved,
just like a tree that's planted by the water
I shall not be moved.

3. On my way to glory, I shall not be moved.
On my way to glory, I shall not be moved,
just like a tree that's planted by the water
I shall not be moved.

4. I'm climbing Jacob's ladder, I shall not be moved.
I'm climbing Jacob's ladder, I shall not be moved,
just like a tree that's planted by the water
I shall not be moved.

5. Old Satan tried to stop me, I shall not be moved.
Old Satan tried to stop me, I shall not be moved,
just like a tree that's planted by the water
I shall not be moved.

Chapter 3

A Universal Question: Who Am I?

What are human beings that
you are mindful of them?
Psalm 8:4*a*

There are good-natured jokes around our home about my notebook. It is a notebook full of questions I want answered when I get to heaven. For example, I want to ask the thief on the cross who said, "Jesus, remember me when you come into your kingdom" (Luke 23:42) if he was a boyhood friend of Jesus. To the best of my knowledge this thief is the only person who ever called Jesus just by his boyhood name. In other instances it is Jesus Christ, Lord Jesus, Jesus Son of David, Teacher, Lord Jesus Christ, and other combinations. I am aware that this is not a deep theological question, by my curiosity level runs high. Questions continue to be added and Bill, my husband, keeps reminding me that these questions will not be important in heaven.

However, there is one person I want to find and ask him about his age when he wrote what is now called Psalm 8. I believe the author had reached what he perceived to be the middle of his life and found he had not fulfilled all his plans. He also must have acknowledged that many of those goals would never be realized. He feels very human. The author sees and appreciates the vastness, order, and beauty of the universe, but in light of such greatness, he sees humans as very insignificant. He feels both the meekness of knowing that we are only dust (Ps. 103:14) and the majesty of that dust being gathered and formed in the image of God (Gen. 1:26). In this dilemma he talks to God about what it means to be created as a human being.

Some believe that asking God questions is wrong, that we should just accept everything "on faith." I would like to propose that questions are the cutting edge of faith development. The opposite of faith is not doubt, it is apathy. It is questions and doubts that move medical science forward in finding cures for and treating disease. Engineers are helped to build stronger and safer buildings because they ask questions and seek greater knowledge. Each life discipline is enhanced when the right questions are asked and pursued. This is certainly true in Christian faith.

Psalm 8 begins with the proclamation of the cosmic sovereignty of God. *The New Interpreter's Bible* states that because of this proclamation Psalm 8 has the distinction of being the first biblical text to reach the moon. The Apollo 11 mission left a silicon disk on the surface containing messages from seventy-three nations, including the Vatican. Psalm 8 was the Vatican's choice for the message.[4]

The psalmist affirms the majesty of God in the creation of the earth and heavens. He seems to be overwhelmed with the cosmic creative sovereignty of God. And rightly so, when we look at a few of the facts:

- Our globe is estimated to weigh six sextillion tons. That is a 6 with 21 zeros.
- The earth is precisely tilted at 23 degrees. If it were any more or less the seasons would be lost. The polar ice cap would melt or increase in size. All life would be affected.
- Our globe revolves a little more than 1,000 miles per hour. In one day we revolve 25,000 miles; in one year over 8 million miles. All life is held in place during these revolutions by the invisible band of gravity that holds us fast.
- Every square yard of the sun emits 130,000 horsepower. That is the equivalent of 450 eight-cylinder engines.
- Our sun is but one minor star in the 100 billion orbs that form the Milky Way.[5]

The list could go on for pages and pages, but let us stop here and affirm with the psalmist:

O LORD, our Sovereign,
how majestic is your name in
all the earth!
You have set your glory above
the heavens. (Ps. 8:1)

Resting Place

REFLECTIONS
Reflect on the beauty you have seen today in nature. Share this with someone else.

PRAYER
Help me, O God, to see the wonder, majesty, and beauty of your creation all around me. Amen.

⌘

Now the focus shifts to humanity. Why does the Creator God, who has brought such beauty, order, and majesty into being, create and care for human beings? "What are human beings that you are mindful of them, mortals that you care for them?" (Ps. 8:4). The central issues of this psalm now become the nature of God and the identity of human beings in relationship to God.

The psalmist comes to realize that humans are a unique creation, made a little lower than God (see Ps. 8:5). And human beings are given royal status (crowned), with glory and honor, which means rule, sovereignty, and dominion over God's creation. This understanding of humanity's creation is also given in Genesis, where the word *dominion* is used:

> Then God said, "Let us make humankind in our image, according to our likeness; and let them have dominion over the fish of the sea, and over the birds of the air, and over the cattle, and over all the wild animals of the earth, and over every creeping thing that creeps upon the earth."
>
> God blessed them, and God said to them, "Be fruitful and multiply, and fill the earth and subdue it; and have dominion over the fish of the sea and over the birds of the air and over every living thing that moves upon the earth." (Gen. 1:26, 28)

In modern terminology, a way of describing glory and honor for humanity would be that each human being is called by God to be like a CEO (Chief Executive Officer) of God's creation. We are each called to care for and protect the creation just as God would. This is the universal calling from God for all humanity.

Resting Place

REFLECTIONS
Take time now to reflect on what the universe would be like if every person accepted the divine call to be the CEO of the arena of the world in which he or she lives.

PRAYER

O God, who created all humanity in your image, may my relationship with you be so bonded that I grow daily into the likeness of your image. Amen.

∽⊃℘⌇∾

If all persons are created "a little less than God," what then, does this mean in the everydayness of life? Let me suggest the following four characteristics.

1. The ability to love and to respond to love. The nature of God is love. The biblical words for love are *heséd* (Old Testament) and *agape* (New Testament). Both mean steadfast love—love that always reaches out toward others, love that never fails. This love forgives, restores, seeks a relationship. It is love that meets people where they are and treats them as they can be. This love is a gift, it cannot be bought or earned—one simply accepts the gift. To love is our nature because of our unique creation. To be otherwise is not what God created us to be.

2. The ability to create beauty and respond to beauty. The creative acts of God reflect God's nature as a designer, creator, and nourisher of beauty. Look at a sunrise, a rose, a baby, or a forest and you see the handiwork of God. Beauty—creation and response—is as necessary to life as oxygen is to the lungs. When we literally "take time to smell the roses" our innermost being feels connected to God our Creator. Medical research offers empirical data to show the effects on the body of creating and responding to beauty; we become healthier individuals and life certainly has greater meaning. Beauty may be created in many ways other than through music, painting, drama, dance, and so on. Beauty can be expressed in a smile, a phone call, a visit, or sharing a meal—beauty is created whenever there is harmony with God, with oneself, and with others.

3. The ability to conceive of justice and pursue it. God is a God of justice. From the opening of the Old Testament to the closing of the New Testament, the justice of God is a ringing theme. In the eighth-century BCE writing of the prophet Amos, God speaks to the nations of Israel and Judah about justice as a way of life. The heart of a relationship with God is the receiving and giving of justice. God challenges the nations and individuals to "let justice roll down like waters, and righteousness like an everflowing stream" (Amos 5:24).

Justice can be said to be the equality of the essentials of life for all persons. A personal friend, Dr. Ted Hill, a medical doctor from

Gallatin, Tennessee, recently wrote a profound article on his Volunteer In Mission trip to Cuautitian Izcalli, Mexico. He was deeply disturbed and challenged by what he saw there, realizing the vast economic, social, and educational inequalities between his American lifestyle and the people of Mexico. He wrote of the importance of seeing the inequities and then working to level the playing field so that others can enjoy the same blessings that we do. Ted's eyes have been opened to injustices. His relationship with God now calls him to be active in eliminating them. He understands the journey. It is hard, demanding, and in stark contrast to his present life. But he is ready to begin!

4. The ability to know God and communicate with God. God seeks to be in relationship with us and humanity's deepest yearning is for such companionship. Saint Augustine describes this need very accurately in the words "Thou hast formed us for Thyself, and our hearts are restless till they find rest in Thee." [6]

Resting Place

REFLECTIONS
Where is God calling you to "level the playing field" for others?

PRAYER
Open my eyes, O God, that I may see others. Open my ears that I may hear others. Open my heart that I may love others. Amen.

The Bible presents the grand sweep of God's seeking nature. Moses met God in the burning bush that was not consumed. Ruth met God at a crisis point in her life. Isaiah experienced God while in the Temple mourning the death of his good friend King Uzziah. Paul met God while on the road to Damascus.

We are made to communicate with God and God seeks the relationship. It is beyond the comprehension of our minds that the One who shapes the heavens, places stars in constellations and star clusters, such as Orion and Pleiades, turns the darkness into a sunrise, and puts a song in a mockingbird, is the same One who seeks to travel with us on our life journey. Indeed, this is amazing grace!

When the Hymnal Committee was working on the 1989 edition

of *The United Methodist Hymnal*, word came out through the media that the hymn "In the Garden" would not be included. One of the reasons given was that the words made God too human and personal. To say "he walks with me, and he talks with me, and he tells me I am his own" diminishes God's nature. Hundreds of letters were sent to the committee giving witness to the fact that God is personal and does, indeed, walk and talk with persons. Their words gave testimony to a personal experience with God that resulted in "the joy we share as we tarry there, none other has ever known."

Whether the Hymnal Committee was considering the removal of "In the Garden," I do not know. But it is included in *The United Methodist Hymnal* (no. 314) and continues to express for some their personal journey with God.

Psalm 8 has profound implications for understanding both God and humanity. The words of this psalm answer for all generations two universal questions: (1) Who is God? and (2) Who am I in relationship to God? The answer comes in the profound truth that God and humans are partners in the care of creation. God shares power, which is very risky. The reputation of God is bound up with the human performance of the universal calling for each person—to be the CEO of all the earth. God, humanity, and all creation are inextricably intertwined.

The psalm closes as it began, "O Lord, our Sovereign, how majestic is your name in all the earth!" (v. 9). But in between is "both an eloquent proclamation of the cosmic sovereignty of God and a remarkable affirmation of the exalted status and vocation of the human creature."[7]

Resting Place

REFLECTIONS FOR JOURNALING
* Describe examples of Creation that are meaningful to you.
* Share with someone how you see your lifestyle as a part of God's vocational call—to manage your area of life as God would have it.
* Write an example from your life of each of the following:
  ❏ The ability to love and respond to love
  ❏ The ability to create beauty and respond to it
  ❏ The ability to conceive of justice and pursue it
  ❏ The ability to know God and communicate with God

PRAYER

Dear Creator, I come to you for re-creation. May your Holy Spirit fill my whole being in such a way that I become an integrated unit of love, beauty, justice, and fellowship with you. Amen.

༺ఞఞ༻

Psalm 8

O LORD our Sovereign,
how majestic is your name in all the earth!
You have set your glory above the heavens.
Out of the mouths of babes and infants
you have founded a bulwark because of your foes,
to silence the enemy and the avenger.
When I look at your heavens, the work of your fingers,
the moon and the stars that you have established;
what are human beings that you are mindful of them,
mortals that you care for them?
Yet you have made them a little lower than God,
and crowned them with glory and honor.
You have given them dominion over the works of your hands;
you have put all things under their feet,
all sheep and oxen,
and also the beasts of the field,
the birds of the air, and the fish of the sea,
whatever passes along the
paths of the seas.
O LORD our Sovereign,
how majestic is your name in all the earth!

Joyful, Joyful, We Adore Thee
Henry Van Dyke, 1907

1. Joyful, joyful, we adore thee, God of glory, Lord of love;
hearts unfold like flowers before thee, opening to the sun above.
Melt the clouds of sin and sadness; drive the dark of doubt away.
Giver of immortal gladness, fill us with the light of day!

2. All thy works with joy surround thee, earth and heaven reflect thy rays,
stars and angels sing around thee, center of unbroken praise.
Field and forest, vale and mountain, flowery meadow, flashing sea,
chanting bird and flowing fountain, call us to rejoice in thee.

3. Thou art giving and forgiving, ever blessing, ever blest,
wellspring of the joy of living, ocean depth of happy rest!
Thou our Father, Christ our brother, all who live in love are thine;
teach us how to love each other, lift us to the joy divine.

4. Mortals, join the mighty chorus which the morning stars began;
love divine is reigning o'er us, binding all within its span.
Ever singing, march we onward, victors in the midst of strife;
joyful music leads us sunward, in the triumph song of life.

Chapter 4

The Lord Is My Shepherd

Surely goodness and mercy shall follow me
all the days of my life.

Psalm 23:6*a*

Certainly the most familiar psalm and possibly the most familiar passage in the entire Bible is Psalm 23. It is quoted as a personal promise, sung in celebration, preached as good news, used at funerals to bring comfort, and prayed through at some of the most critical points in our lives as a rock to which we can cling. This psalm is loved because, perhaps more than any other psalm, it meets people where they are in their life's journey. The Twenty-third Psalm presents a shepherd who shows us the right way through life, protects us, provides for us, renews us, and, most of all, loves us.

As we meditate on this psalm I would like for us to focus on the role of a Middle Eastern shepherd. Most Americans know very little about sheep and shepherds. In the time frame of Psalm 23 everyone knew about shepherds for it was an honored profession. When the psalmist wrote Psalm 23 he was using language and describing a profession to which everyone in his time and culture could relate.

The psalm begins with the announcement, "The LORD is my shepherd, I shall not want." Immediately a new insight is given. In ancient times people were of worth only as members of a tribe, family, or nation—never as individuals. The psalmist uses the personal pronoun "my," indicating a personal relationship with the shepherd (God). Martin Luther once said that you can tell the nature of a religion by its personal pronouns. Such pronouns are definitely present in this psalm, indicating that a personal relationship is established between the shepherd and his sheep—between God and individuals.

Resting Place

REFLECTIONS
What do you feel in your soul when you read, "The Lord is MY shepherd"?

PRAYER
Dear Shepherd of the flock, thank you for your constant care and personal concerns for my highest good. Amen.

The opening verse of the psalm, "The Lord is my shepherd, I shall not want," is really a summary of what is to come. It is like a topic sentence in a paragraph or a theorem in geometry. Because the Lord is my shepherd the following lifestyle can be expected:

1. **"He makes me lie down in green pastures."** Sheep are like me; they will keep eating even though they are full. However, the shepherd keeps close watch. When a sheep has eaten enough, the shepherd will hold his staff by the bottom end and place the crook end of the staff around the sheep's hind leg and pull it to the ground. Then he will gently pat the head of the sheep as a way of saying, "Relax, enjoy what you have eaten, there is more. It is a green pasture, do not be anxious."

You and I can certainly relate to this. We have times like this when life is going along well, we are full of happiness, contentment, and good living. All of a sudden we are made to lie down. It may be the result of an accident, health, death of a loved one, loss of a job, or heartache over children; the list is endless. Such times are frightening to say the least. If we follow the shepherd, we, too, will feel the pat of the shepherd's staff saying "I am with you. As bad as this seems it can be a green pasture time. We are together in this."

Paul understood such a relationship with Jesus when he wrote, "We know that all things work together for good for those who love God, who are called according to his purpose" (Rom. 8:28). Notice Paul did not say "all things are good," for this is certainly not evident in this world. But all things can work together for good for those who love God. The events of September 11, 2001 were certainly not good, but God has brought good out of them in many ways. We have seen our fellow citizens realize the

24

value of life, share their resources, engage in acts of selflessness, reflect on what is really important, and begin to seek answers in the church. May the tragedies of September 11 bring persons into a deeper understanding of one another, the root causes behind the terror, and a commitment to be part of the solution to help God establish a world of justice, mercy, and righteousness. Such a response would be a "green pasture" time, but a time that will not minimize the pain of that tragic day. God, our Shepherd, feels the pain we all felt on September 11—just as a shepherd grieves over a lost sheep. Such an understanding of the nature of God is not found in any other world religion.

I was teaching a seminar on "Faith Is a Journey, Never a Destination." At the close of the session a woman came to me and said, "I believe all religions are a pathway to the same God." My response was simply "Oh!" She continued by stating that she felt it did not matter what you believed just as long as you were faithful to your beliefs. I asked her if she would do something for me. After a lengthy discussion in which I would not identify what I would ask her to do, she agreed that she would. Back in my office I listed the thirteen major world religions along with some questions for her to use in comparing and contrasting these religions. These included inquiries into the nature of the Deity, the creation of humankind, the root cause of evil in the world, how one comes into relationship with the Deity, and the teachings about life after death.

Weeks went by and I did not receive an answer. I became concerned for fear our relationship had been broken. Finally, a one-sentence letter arrived. It said, "Evelyn, I give up." I prayed that through a study of the major world religions, a new understanding of the unique nature of God as revealed in Jesus Christ had been grasped. That she then realized that all religions are not the pathway to the same God. Such an exploration is of vital importance because what we think about God affects how we feel about ourselves, others, and our relationship with the universe.

Resting Place

REFLECTIONS

Describe the nature of God as you understand God. Is this consistent with what Jesus taught?

O God, thank you for being who you are, a God of love, mercy, justice, and grace. Help me to be open to you in all areas of my life. Amen.

⌘

2. God, who is like a shepherd, "leads me beside still waters." Sheep are, by instinct, frightened by fast running water or what is commonly referred to as whitewater. However, they have no innate fear of deep water that is calm on the surface. This can be a fatal situation for the sheep because, when wet, the wool on the sheep's body becomes very heavy, and thus the sheep is unable to swim. Sheep need a good shepherd who will guide them by "still waters." So do we. There are dangers around us everyday and we need our Good Shepherd to guide us to safety. Like sheep who do not recognize still water as a danger, the most threatening dangers in our life are very possibly the ones we never see or those we do not recognize.

An old gospel song tells a story about God allowing a drunk driver to run out of gas before hitting someone head-on. That song illustrates God, the Good Shepherd, leading us beside the still waters. Because of decisions we make or events forced upon us, Christians die in unexpected situations every day, but even then it is the ultimate blessing to know that we are with the Good Shepherd, who will lead us to a new sheepfold that very night.

Resting Place

REFLECTIONS
- Remember a time in your life when you were led "beside still waters."
- Do you allow the shepherd to lead you each day to the deep pool of water?

PRAYER

O God, who guides me like a shepherd, I surrender this day to your leadership. Amen.

⌘

26

3. **In our lives we encounter situations that reach out to consume us, similar to the deep pools that are traps for the sheep.** These situations might be worry over children, money, health, death, friends, clothes, or home. Can you add others to the list? We fear the loss of a job, growing old, children moving away, the future, and change. If we will allow it, the Shepherd will lead us beside still waters, to the place where we can drink from God's pool of unconditional love, which brings serenity at the center of our being and rest from carrying the heavy load of fear.

4. **"He restores my soul."** The land of Israel is covered with large and small rocks that can easily cause a sheep to stumble or fall. The shepherd responds quickly to fallen sheep as he takes the crook end of his staff, puts it over the head of the sheep and lifts it to safe ground. This is called "restoring the sheep." One of my favorite pictures of a shepherd is one in which the shepherd has one foot on top of the cliff, the other in a strained position off the cliff, and in his right hand he is using his staff to rescue the sheep. The eyes of the sheep are filled with confidence in the shepherd. Overhead the birds of prey are circling—waiting to dive, first to blind the animal, then to return for the body. This picture vividly shows the rescue of the fallen sheep.

Sheep may be found in other predicaments that require the rescue called "restoring the sheep." A "cast down" sheep is one that is lying on its back and is not able to get up on its own strength. If the shepherd does not come to the rescue the sheep will exhaust itself by kicking its legs in the air as it tries to move its body into a standing position. The good shepherd is on alert for a cast down sheep and seeks to quickly restore the sheep to the flock.

In several psalms the shepherd's term "cast down" refers to persons who are spiritually drained and feel helpless and hopeless about a life situation. An example is found in Psalm 42:11: "Why are you cast down, O my soul, and why are you disquieted within me? Hope in God; for I shall again praise him, my help and my God." How comforting for us to know that the restoration of our soul is God's ultimate desire for us. I recently saw an example of "he restores my soul" in the church I attend, Long's Chapel United Methodist Church. A young man named Frank who at one time attended the church was now in prison. While there he accepted Christ as his Savior and before his release he wrote our pastor, stating that he felt remorse for his crimes. He further wondered if the congregation would accept him and asked if he could join the church when he was released from prison.

The pastor shared the letter with the congregation. Members began to write to Frank telling him how happy they were that he would soon be released and invited him to be a member of the church family. When that special Sunday arrived, at every entrance to the church there were colorful balloons attached to large signs that read, "Welcome Home, Frank." What a living witness to "he restores my soul."

Resting Place

REFLECTIONS
- Why do you feel "cast down" at times?
- Do you allow God to restore your soul?

PRAYER
O Lord, help me to remember that when the storms of life are raging, you are with me. I am not alone. Amen.

5. **"He leads me in right paths for his name's sake."** This could also be correctly written, "He leads me in right paths for his reputation's sake." As in all professions, shepherds have reputations. When in Israel, it is interesting to be where shepherds are bringing their flocks in to spend the night. After the sheep are cared for the shepherds talk about the day. If a shepherd has lost a sheep he is questioned: Did you search the caves? Did you find the body? What killed the sheep? Such questions tell of the accountability expected from the shepherds. This is how a shepherd builds or loses his reputation.

This verse affirms that the psalmist has found the character of God to be trustworthy—God has led him in right paths and in God's provision all his needs are met. These needs are not what our consumer-oriented society would find adequate, but to the psalmist they are all he wants: green pasture; still water; a place to rest and sleep—the shepherd's presence.

When standing in a grocery story checkout line I read the front pages of magazines that are in the nearby rack. These pages have titillating headlines to grab your attention and entice you to purchase the magazine. Almost every issue has a feature on stress—its causes, cures, and the latest thoughts on reducing the amount of stress we feel. When doing an overview of the stories you will notice that the same causes for stress are listed again and again: clutter, being over-scheduled, trying to live up to impossible expectations, credit card debt, too little sleep, the need for a personal time to be alone—to list just a few. The primary suggestion offered is to simplify your lifestyle. The editors of these magazines carefully miss the point that "clever advertisers have succeeded in convincing us that what former generations considered incredible luxuries are now basic necessities."[8] To say it another way, we follow the wrong shepherd.

Resting Place

REFLECTIONS
• What are your barest necessities?
• Where would you begin in order to simplify your lifestyle?

PRAYER
Forgive me, O God, for allowing the world to shape me in its mold. I want to trust and obey you for I now know that there is no other way. I rest my life in you. Amen.

6. **"Even though I walk through the darkest valley, I fear no evil for you are with me."** The Valley of the Shadow of Death or Valley of the Shadow refers to a real place in Israel—a location that is believed to be referenced in this verse. It is a narrow passageway through which a shepherd must pass to get the sheep from the sheepfold to good pasture. As the shepherd and sheep get near the entrance the sheep sense danger, for often predators are hidden in the large boulders. The sheep stay very close to the shepherd. He moves slowly with small steps while calling each sheep by name. The sheep will go through the valley because the shepherd is with them.

This section of Psalm 23 is associated with dying, death, and the funeral service. I would like to suggest that it is also relevant to daily living. Life experiences bring us face-to-face with the need to go through the Valley of the Shadow. The loss of a job, divorce, accidents, the death of a dream, a child born with a limited physical body, and foreclosure on your home are all Valleys of the

Shadow. The psalmist affirms that we do not go through any life experience alone; the shepherd goes with us—leading us, calling us by name, giving encouragement to move on, and caring deeply. The chorus found in "Because He Lives" expresses this relationship meaningfully:

> Because he lives, I can face tomorrow;
> because he lives, all fear is gone.[9]

Of course, it is also appropriate to remember this Psalm in the midst of dying and death. While I served as one of the chaplains at Emory University, a very sick woman from South Georgia was admitted to the hospital. She knew her chance for earthly survival was small and she wanted to talk about her life and her death. We talked about things that women share—husbands, children, grandchildren, home, church—and our friendship deepened. We quoted scripture and shared our faith journeys. One day she asked, "Will you be with me when I die?" I assured her I would be there. She responded, "If possible, I want to share what is happening with you." This was a statement I had heard from several persons. It seems that as we approach death there comes a great desire to share what has greatest meaning to us so that others may know Truth.

The day came when I was paged to her room. When I entered she took my left hand. Her words were clear and strong, "I feel such love as I have never felt before." Then she asked a question, "Do you hear the choir?" I didn't but her face was responding to the heavenly choir. She continued sharing this holy moment with "Look at the flowers." Then her right hand began to reach toward the heavens and she said, "Why, there's Jesus." At this moment she was released from a tired sick body to the imperishable resurrected body. In her life and in her death she was with the Good Shepherd.

Resting Place

REFLECTIONS

We are not physical beings having a spiritual experience. We are spiritual beings having a human experience. Reflect on the reality that our spirit is eternal. We carry eternity within us now.

࿆

7. "Your rod and your staff—they comfort me." The rod is a shepherd's tool approximately three feet long and three inches thick, which the good shepherd used for protection from wild animals as well as for the clearing of overgrown paths. The wooden rod also signifies royal dominion and authority. The psalmist is stating that God is an authority and power, and also provides for our lives. The rod is a defensive weapon against many perils and would be vital to the flock's preservation. The sheep would not be intimidated by the sight of the rod in the good shepherd's hand, but rather, they would feel comfort from its presence.

The importance of the staff has already been mentioned in the rescue of a sheep that has fallen over the cliff or is cast down. It was also used to pull down a tree limb so that the sheep could nibble the green leaves. The staff is comforting because it protects and provides for the sheep. These images give us another way to describe God's providential care and protection of our lives.

Resting Place

REFLECTIONS
- What are some of the tools that God uses now for the protection and care of our lives?
- Spend time remembering a recent experience of God caring for you.

PRAYER
"Let your steadfast love come to me, O LORD, your salvation according to your promise." Amen. (Ps. 119:41)

࿆

8. "You prepare a table before me in the presence of my enemies." Almost everyone in the Middle East even to this day is familiar with the shepherd's phrase "preparing a table." Before a shepherd takes his sheep to new grazing ground he goes over every square inch of the ground looking for the enemies of the sheep, which range from poisonous weeds to the deadly cobra. The weeds are pulled and destroyed, the cobra den demolished, and the snakes killed by the shepherd—the table is then prepared for the sheep to come and eat without fear.

What beautiful imagery for us. God goes before us and prepares the way for our coming. We can move into tomorrow without fear of what might be present. Our role is to totally trust the God who is like a shepherd. Isn't this what Jesus was saying in the Sermon on the Mount? "Therefore, do not worry, saying, 'What will we eat?' or 'What will we drink?' or 'What will we wear?'. . . indeed your heavenly Father knows that you need all these things" (Matt. 6:31-32).

Resting Place

REFLECTIONS
• What keeps us from placing our total trust in God?
• Share with someone a recent example of God preparing the table before you.

PRAYER
"Though the fig tree does not blossom, and no fruit is on the vines; though the produce of the olive fails and the fields yield no food; though the flock is cut off from the fold and there is no herd in the stalls, yet I will rejoice in the LORD; I will exult in the God of my salvation." Amen. (Hab. 3:17)

9. "You anoint my head with oil; my cup overflows." This powerful affirmation of God's care comes from the way a shepherd puts his sheep into the fold in the evening. As sheep forage, their forehead pushes the thorny bushes back so they can reach grass hidden under the bush's limbs. This causes many scratches and puncture wounds to their head. The good shepherd has his cup of oil at the gate of the sheepfold. As the flock enters he dips his fingers in the cup of oil and, calling each sheep by name, he anoints the hurts of the day to bring healing—as much from his touch as from the oil.

So it is with God. Daily living brings with it many scratches, but there is oil in the hand of God to "make the wounded whole."

Resting Place

REFLECTIONS
- Each evening as you are ready to go to sleep, allow God to rub oil on the wounds of the day so they will heal during sleep.

PRAYER
Dear Shepherd, I come to you with my hurts, my scratches, my needs. Let me feel your healing oil as it penetrates my being. I want to be healed, O God. Amen.

⌘

10. "Surely goodness and mercy shall follow me all the days of my life, and I shall dwell in the house of the LORD my whole life long." In the beginning of our journey through the Twenty-third Psalm, we saw that the personal pronoun "my" was used often. Indeed the psalm begins in this way, "The LORD is my shepherd." But it concludes with "being in the house of the LORD forever"—experiencing God on the communal level.

Following the Good Shepherd will bring personal care, food, water, rest, guidance, and protection, but we are not alone—we are part of God's flock. God cares for all with the same love. As we experience this care we become open to others in God's family realizing that God loves all and seeks a relationship with all. God extends an open invitation to all persons to become family in the household, to truly come home. The psalmist accepts the invitation with joy and knows he will live there "my whole life long."

Resting Place

REFLECTIONS FOR JOURNALING
- What does it mean to be "at home"?
- In what ways is the invitation to come home extended?
- Write about your journey home.

PRAYER
Good Shepherd, when I am tired, when I am weak, when I am worn out from my wandering in the night and through the storm, then take my hand, precious Lord, and lead me home. Amen.

Psalm 23

The LORD is my shepherd, I shall not want.
  He makes me lie down in green pastures;
he leads me beside still waters;
  he restores my soul.
He leads me in right paths
  for his name's sake.
Even though I walk through the darkest valley,
  I fear no evil;
for you are with me;
  your rod and your staff—they comfort me.
You prepare a table before me
  in the presence of my enemies;
you anoint my head with oil;
  my cup overflows.
Surely goodness and mercy shall follow me
  all the days of my life,
and I shall dwell in the house of the LORD
  my whole life long.

The Lord's My Shepherd, I'll Not Want
Words from the Scottish Psalter, 1650

1. The Lord's my shepherd, I'll not want.
   He makes me down to lie
   in pastures green; he leadeth me
   the quiet waters by.

2. My soul he doth restore again,
   and me to walk doth make
   within the paths of righteousness,
   e'en for his own name's sake.

3. Yea, though I walk in death's dark vale,
   yet will I fear no ill;
   for thou art with me, and thy rod
   and staff me comfort still.

4. My table thou has furnished
   in presence of my foes;
   my head thou dost with oil anoint,
   and my cup overflows.

5. Goodness and mercy all my life
   shall surely follow me;
   and in God's house forevermore
   my dwelling place shall be.

Chapter 5

Can You Hear Me, Lord?

Purge me with hyssop, and I shall be clean;
wash me, and I shall be whiter than snow.
Psalm 51:7

A guilty conscience is a terrible companion. Sleep becomes difficult; food does not digest well; thoughts are very susceptible to the evil one; relationships suffer; our communication with God seems impossible, cold, and distant. When guilt is raging through our system, we feel alone and desolate.

Imagine the guilt you would experience if you had participated in an extramarital affair. Imagine you are the beloved leader of a great nation, and you ignored the sacred bonds pledged between you, your spouse, and God when you found someone to whom you were physically attracted. Imagine that you chose momentary pleasure over the sacred relationship and further imagine the impact this would have on you and on your spouse. Imagine all of this has happened and you still want to continue the relationship with your spouse but also with this new, exciting person. One problem arises though; this new, exciting person has a spouse. Something must be done to protect you—after all, you are the leader of the country. So you have the spouse killed in a battle. King David did not have to imagine—he did all this in his affair with Bathsheba.

King David, the king with a heart for God, carried out the events listed above. He broke at least half of the Ten Commandments, including the ones prohibiting adultery and murder. In timing that we will never begin to understand, David's conscience finally reached his soul. The weight of what he had done was more than he could bear and in his agony, as part of his healing, he turned to God in prayer. We hear this cry in Psalm 51, a prayer for help. Listen to a broken heart pleading for healing in the first five verses:

> Have mercy on me, O God,
>   according to your steadfast love;
> according to your abundant mercy
>   blot out my transgressions.

35

Wash me thoroughly from my iniquity,
and cleanse me from my sin.
For I know my transgressions,
and my sin is ever before me.
Against you, you alone, have I sinned,
and done what is evil in your sight,
so that you are justified in your sentence
and blameless when you pass judgment.
Indeed, I was born guilty,
a sinner when my mother conceived me. (Ps. 51:1-5)

Several things are important in what King David is saying; first, notice that he brings nothing to the table except the sin. He is counting on God's unfailing love, God's great compassion to blot out the stain of his sin. Next, he recognizes his sin; his shameful deeds are keeping him awake, haunting him at night, and overshadowing the events of the day. He realizes that his sin is against God's will and that it is now separating him from God. For someone who had previously been in an intimate relationship with God, he must have felt alienated from his source of joy, power, and life. And it was his fault. What a burden!

One part of this has always been of special interest to me. In verse 5, King David shows us that he was as human as we are—he makes an excuse. He wants to remind God that he was born a sinner, even from the moment his mother conceived him. Original sin is over us all until forgiven through the blood of Jesus. Since the Messiah was yet to come, David did not have the blessing that we have; the tree that would become the cross was not yet even growing. But David wants to remind God, "Hey, I was born a sinner and this is just a continuation of that condition." Maybe David wanted to echo Psalm 103:14: "For he knows how we were made; he remembers that we are dust." I have found comfort in the fact that even the great King David wanted to make an excuse for his actions. Am I ready to surrender my excuses and deal with reality?

Resting Place

REFLECTIONS
Identify excuses you use to justify certain actions.

PRAYER
O God, in this hour, grant me the courage to stop using excuses and claim who I am—your creation. Amen.

∼ↄᏮᏎ∽

In verse 6, the psalm makes a transition, from begging for mercy to David's realization that the sin is not acceptable to God and that God desires honesty in our souls. Then David takes us into his requests for God to fix the condition inside of David that allows him to sin.

> Purge me with hyssop, and I shall be clean;
> wash me, and I shall be whiter than snow.
> Let me hear joy and gladness;
> let the bones that you have crushed rejoice.
> Hide your face from my sins,
> and blot out all my iniquities. (Ps. 51:7-9)

As King David is writing these verses, the cleansing and renewal has begun. In the middle of the cleansing, the guilt returns and David is embarrassed by his sin. He is embarrassed that God is able to perceive the condition in him that allowed the sin and the actions it creates. David asks God to stop looking at his sins. He misses the relationship he once had with God and his only desire now is for that relationship to be restored, for David to again hear joy. "Yes," David surrenders and says, "God, you have won, the weight of living without you is more than I can bear, please blot out my iniquities."

Verses 10 through 11 are great petitions to God from David. He is saying to God, "Look Lord, I do not want to live this way. Please give me a heart that is not filled with the sin I have created. Create in me a new heart and give me, once again, a righteous spirit. Lord, I have sinned, but please do not abandon me or leave me."

Verse 12 touches us now with the profound feelings David must have had when he wrote it thousands of years ago: "Restore to me again the joy of your salvation, and make me willing to obey you." In this verse we sense the yearning of David for the once-felt experience of salvation (wholeness of life), but he knows this is not possible without obedience to God. At this point he asks God to make him willing to obey. He realizes that he may be the king of Israel, but he is not able to rule his actions; God's power is absolutely necessary for obedience to be carried out in his life. The joy of having that salvation in our lives is overwhelming; David forgot that for a period of time or maybe he just took it for granted. Maybe we do also. Many of you can remember the joy you felt the moments after you committed your life to Jesus and experienced the forgiveness of sins. David needed to feel that way again. So do we. Daily we must follow David's example and ask for forgiveness and restoration of our relationship with God; we must ask God to fill us with joy. With all the problems around us it is a tremendous blessing to feel, deep in our bones, the joy of God's salvation personalized in our soul.

Resting Place

REFLECTIONS

Think about the power of repentance. It opens a new world for us—a world of living in God's awesome love.

PRAYER

O God, I come to you asking that you will forgive my sin (name the sin) and that you will create in me a clean heart and renew a right spirit within me. Amen.

In verses 13-15, David tells God that he will be a public witness to God's work in his life. His clean heart and new spirit will be accompanied by outwardly visible and audible proclamation. Every organ of speech will participate: tongue, lips, and mouth (vv. 14-15). God does not require a bargaining for the cleansing of souls and King David was fully aware of that fact. I believe David's heart for God was such that this was a natural response to the cleansing he believed was to come. As any pastor will tell you, often the best witness for the cleansing power of Jesus is someone who has just experienced that cleansing. Listen to the message from Jesus as recorded in Luke: "A certain creditor had two debtors; one owed five hundred denarii, and the other fifty. When they could not pay, he canceled the debts for both of them. Now which of them will love him more?" Simon answered, "I suppose the one for whom he canceled the greater debt." And Jesus said to him, "You have judged rightly. . . . Therefore, I tell you, her sins, which were many, have been forgiven; hence she has shown great love. But the one to whom little is forgiven, loves little" (Luke 7:41-43, 47).

Most of us have not plotted the death of a person or had an extramarital affair, but we all have sins that once haunted us day and night. Psalm 51 certainly calls to our attention the universal feature of humanity—sin. It also reminds us that sin has consequences; the first child born to Bathsheba died and David's family nearly fell apart. Nevertheless, David's sin was forgiven; he was allowed to live and to hold the position of king.

However, Psalm 51 is not just bad news about human nature, it is also the good news about God's nature. The good news is that by the grace of God disobedient, rebellious, conniving persons may become partners with God. Grace does not excuse sin, but it treasures the sinner. Saul, the one who gave silent assent for the stoning of Stephen, became Paul, an apostle of Jesus Christ. Matthew, a civil servant who was a tax collector (a profession known for greed and held in contempt by other Jews), became one of the Twelve. Grace is God's initiative on our behalf. Each of us could add our names to the list, telling who we were and who we are now through the grace of God.

Resting Place

REFLECTIONS

Remember a time when you received from God a gift of grace.
- How did this gift affect your life?
- Share with someone an experience in which you were the giver of grace.

PRAYER

The gift of your grace, O God, is all I need to have a life of joy, meaning, and service to others. May I open my life to receive this gift. Amen.

David has asked God to blot out the stain of his sins, to cleanse him from guilt, to purify him, to wash him whiter than snow, to stop looking at his sins, and to remove the stain of his guilt (v. 14). But the guilt is still present in David's heart. David is still asking for cleansing and forgiveness. We should never underestimate the power of evil and the impact and influence it has on our lives. I have heard evil compared to pounding nails into a board. Later you can pull the nails out, but the scars always remain.

Verses 16 and 17 are beautiful in their acknowledgment of what God wants from us. God does not want animal sacrifices, but the sacrifice of "a broken and contrite heart." God desires our willingness to give our whole self to God's will. God wants us to have a spirit of openness, not a spirit of pride. God desires for us to commit our all for God's glory and for our ultimate benefit.

Resting Place

REFLECTIONS FOR JOURNALING
- Visualize what could happen if the Israelis and the Palestinians received and gave God's grace to one another. Imagine the same for the Catholics and Protestants in Northern Ireland.
- Visualize what could happen in families if all could give grace to one another.
- How would the universal church be different if all were dispensers of God's grace?

PRAYER
"Search me, O God, and know my heart; test me and know my thoughts. See if there is any wicked way in me, and lead me in the way everlasting." Amen. (Ps. 139:23-24)

Psalm 51

Have mercy on me, O God,
    according to your steadfast love;
according to your abundant mercy
    blot out my transgressions.
Wash me thoroughly from my iniquity,
    and cleanse me from my sin.
For I know my transgressions,
    and my sin is ever before me.
Against you, you alone, have I sinned,
    and done what is evil in your sight,
so that you are justified in your sentence
    and blameless when you pass judgment.
Indeed, I was born guilty,
    a sinner when my mother conceived me.
You desire truth in the inward being;
    therefore teach me wisdom in my secret heart.
Purge me with hyssop, and I shall be clean;

wash me, and I shall be whiter than snow.
Let me hear joy and gladness;
   let the bones that you have crushed rejoice.
Hide your face from my sins,
   and blot out all my iniquities.
Create in me a clean heart, O God,
   and put a new and right spirit within me.
Do not cast me away from your presence,
   and do not take your holy spirit from me.
Restore to me the joy of your salvation,
   and sustain in me a willing spirit.
Then will I teach transgressors your ways,
   and sinners will return to you.
Deliver me from bloodshed, O God,
   O God of my salvation,
   and my tongue will sing aloud of your deliverance.
O Lord, open my lips,
   and my mouth will declare your praise.
For you have no delight in sacrifice;
   if I were to give a burnt offering, you would not be pleased.
The sacrifice acceptable to God is a broken spirit;
   a broken and contrite heart,
   O God, you will not despise.
Do good to Zion in your good pleasure;
   rebuild the walls of Jerusalem,
then you will delight in right sacrifices,
   in burnt offerings and whole burnt offerings;
   then bulls will be offered on your altar.

O For a Heart to Praise My God
Charles Wesley, 1742

1. O for a heart to praise my God,
a heart from sin set free,
a heart that always feels thy blood
so freely shed for me.

2. A heart resigned, submissive, meek,
my great Redeemer's throne,
where only Christ is heard to speak,
where Jesus reigns alone.

3. A humble, lowly, contrite heart,
believing, true, and clean,
which neither life nor death can part
from Christ who dwells within.

4. A heart in every thought renewed
and full of love divine,
perfect and right and pure and good,
a copy, Lord, of thine.

5. Thy nature, gracious Lord, impart;
come quickly from above;
write thy new name upon my heart,
thy new, best name of Love.

Chapter 6

An Attitude of Gratitude

Praise the LORD, I tell myself; with my whole heart,
I will praise his holy name.

Psalm 103:1 (NLT)

Years ago I found that praise music spoke my heart's cry very strongly. Today I continue to feel close to God when singing praise music, especially while walking in the woods or around Lake Junaluska, North Carolina. I understand why Psalm 103 is one of the most familiar and most beloved of all the psalms.

One day the thought came to me, "Why does God need our praise?" The more I thought about this, the more restless my heart became. Finally, a dear friend shared with me that praise is for God, who deserves our praise, but it is also for us. It reminds us of the blessings God has shared with us. It reminds us of God's love for us and the fact that God needed us, and sought the relationship. In *This Is Christianity*, Maxie Dunnam wrote, "As Dionysius argued in the fourth century, God created us because God 'yearned' to love us."[10] We are made in God's image for such a relationship. What greater blessing can there be than this?

Psalm 103, believed to be written by David, the shepherd and the king, is a psalm of praise that is overflowing from the heart. The psalmist knew that God was his Creator, his Reason for existence, his Sustenance during life, his Healer, his Savior, his Forgiver, and his Salvation. I pray that at some point in my Christian walk I can feel God as intimately as the psalmist felt when writing these words. When arriving at this point, how can we be quiet and not praise God?

The word *bless* appears throughout the Psalms. This word seems to have originally meant "to bend the knee before—that is, to bow in homage to one's sovereign."[11] Let us look at some of the reasons the psalmist gives for blessing God.

Even as Christians, our lives are not all mountaintop experiences. In verse 3 we are reminded that God "forgives all my sins and heals all my diseases" (NLT). We, as Christians, are forgiven, but many of us are still inflicted by disease. How can we praise God for healing us when we are still suffering? You can hear the pain in people who have lost a loved one to cancer or other diseases as they ask God, "Why?" You can hear the pain of a person with a debilitating disease as they read these words and are in worse physical condition today than yesterday.

As the Reverend Billy Graham said at the National Prayer Breakfast in Washington D.C. several years ago, "I have read the end of the Book. I know how it ends—GOD WINS!" Yes, we have afflictions that hinder us, but God can do one of two things, heal us or use us. With God's comfort and strength we can choose to use our physical problems for the glory of God.

My husband Bill has arthritis in his legs and feet and the effects of this disease have been traumatic. For a decade now he has been unable to walk any substantial distance and all walking is painful. The best doctors and medicines are helpful but the problem persists. Prayer has helped Bill to cope with and accept the situation and his attitude is "full speed ahead!" His ministry has become one of support in my travels and teaching and he is an inspiration for many who might stay at home otherwise. He reminds us all that there are things to do, people to meet, praises to sing, and that we should always wonder, "What is around the next curve?" An attitude of gratitude is the key. The apostle Paul knew this well: "He comforts us in all our troubles so that we can comfort others. When others are troubled, we will be able to give them the same comfort God has given us" (2 Cor. 1:4 NLT). Bill has a unique ministry of giving comfort to others because he knows pain; he can illustrate by his own life that physical limitations do not limit love, joy, friendship, hope, and opportunity for ministry.

Two years ago our son Bill, Jr. was diagnosed with diabetes. An improper diet and lack of exercise led him to the point that his body responded with this disease; the disease did not come from God. No disease does. But, very thankfully, many years ago God gave researchers the tools to allow him to control the glucose level in his system. By following the physical laws God created—correcting his diet, getting enough exercise, and using the God-given medicines doctors prescribe, Bill is experiencing a good life.

Verse 3 states that God heals all diseases. We have talked of controlling and coping with disease, but not necessarily healing disease. In fact, God heals through doctors, nurses, medicine, and also through God's own healing touch. I have experienced all of these. You have also. Praise God! One day, the Ultimate Healer will heal each of us from a limited body to a resurrected body. We will dance together in the streets of heaven after God has brought us from this body of dust (verse 14) to the spiritual body. Paul gives us this promise: "But it is not the spiritual that is first, but the physical, and then the spiritual" (1 Cor. 15:46).

In the meantime, we say with the psalmist: "Bless the LORD, O my soul, and all that is within me, bless his holy name" (v. 1). My prayer is that all of us are open to God's daily message to us and that God's glory is reflected in us each moment in this life, until we are face-to-face with that glory in heaven.

REFLECTIONS
- Do I get up each morning with a song of praise in my heart?
- Do I praise God through the day regardless of the circumstances?
- Make a list of reasons you have to offer praise to God.

PRAYER
"Praise the LORD! Praise the LORD, O my soul! I will praise the LORD as long as I live; I will sing praises to my God all my life long." Amen. (Ps. 146:1-2)

Another reason the psalmist gives for praise is God's steadfast love and mercy. In several verses these two qualities of God's nature are listed (vv. 4, 8, 11, 17). To experience these is to have the deepest need and yearning of humankind met to the fullest. These are gifts from God—they cannot be bought, earned by good works, or given through selection. They are part of God's nature and are available to all persons. God's steadfast love seeks a permanent relationship in all lives. God's mercy, defined as "entering into our being and giving us what we need, not what we deserve," is offered to all. These divine attributes are God with us.

Several years ago extensive surgery made it necessary for me to stay at home for three months. This was a difficult limitation for me. One day as I was having a "pity party," the door of our condo opened. There stood our son Bill, Jr., who is 6 feet 4 inches tall, and his best friend, Ward Jackson, who is the same height. These two were holding a doll that I later learned was called The Jesus Doll.[12] My response to the scene at the door was, "Are you two OK? You look odd standing there with the doll." Their response was that they were fine but they sensed that I was not. When your son tells you this you realize that you need to listen, so I did. Bill, Jr. said, "Mom, I think you have forgotten something very important and that is that God's steadfast love and mercy are always offered to you. Ward and I brought you The Jesus Doll to remind you that God is with you, Jesus is with you, and the Holy Spirit is with you. Therefore, there is no need for a 'pity party.'" This message was a gift from God.

The Jesus Doll is a blessing to me. The doll sits in a little rocking chair in our living room. But there are times when The Jesus Doll goes to a sick child, a bereaved adult, or a teaching event. Persons may leave in Jesus' lap their written needs or prayers. I can now understand and sing with the psalmist, "Bless the LORD, O my soul, and do not forget all his benefits . . . who crowns you with steadfast love and mercy" (vv. 2, 4b).

Resting Place

REFLECTIONS
- What would you like to say to Jesus right now? He is with you, ready to listen.
- Make a conscious effort to focus daily on the fact that Jesus said, "I am with you always even to the end of the age." Am I open for this relationship every day?

PRAYER
O Christ, you offer yourself to us each day. I often say "no" to the relationship. In repentance and faith I come again asking for your presence to be my guide for the day. Amen.

Another reason the psalmist gives for praising God is found in verse 5: the joy-filled life is a renewing life. With the attitude of gratitude comes the renewal of our soul so that we are able to soar like the eagle. I thank the psalmist for this beautiful image of human restoration. Many of us have seen eagles soaring in the heavens and have been in awe of this marvelous capability.

Soaring comes into reality as the eagle faces the strong storm currents, spreads its massive wings, and allows the wind currents to lift it above the storm. So it is with persons who face the storm(s) of life and allow God's power to raise them above the storm. The psalmist mentions God's awesome care in several storms of life.

- "The LORD works vindication and justice for all who are oppressed. He made known his ways to Moses, his acts to the people of Israel. The LORD is merciful and gracious, slow to anger and abounding in steadfast love" (vv. 6-8).
- "He does not deal with us according to our sins, nor repay us according to our iniquities" (v. 10).
- "As far as the east is from the west, so far he removes our transgressions from us" (v. 12).

Yes, humans can soar in life because of God's nature. The psalmist allows us to know the very heart of God, which is steadfast love, compassion, forgiveness, and mercy.

However, while Psalm 103 communicates God's steadfast love, there seems to be qualifications. Three times the psalmist reserves steadfast love or compassion for those who fear God, while righteousness is reserved for those who are obedient (vv. 11, 13, 17, 18). This may seem to be a contradiction, but as members of the human family we can understand this. Every loving parent knows the tensions that are present in raising children. There is both the absolute necessity for obedience and the willingness to extend steadfast love and forgiveness. Both are essential for the welfare of the child. It cannot be otherwise for God. God's grace is found both in requiring obedience and in extending steadfast love.

Resting Place

REFLECTIONS
- How is accountability related to steadfast love?
- Can you think of examples from Christ's teachings of the relationship between obedience and steadfast love?

PRAYER
O Covenant God, who calls us to obedient and righteous living, forgive us for not being faithful to this call. We want to renew our covenant with you at this time. Please accept us and give us your steadfast love and mercy. Amen.

At the United Methodist college where I taught, one semester of Bible study was required for graduation. This meant I had students who were in class because they chose to come; others were there because they had to come. One who came because he had to was Broderick. Broderick was about 6 feet 6 inches tall, weighed over 300 pounds and enjoyed being the last one to come in the room and the first one to leave. On his first test Broderick made a score of 27. I wrote a note on the test paper that said, "Broderick, I want you to come see me today. If you do not, I'm coming after you."

That afternoon Broderick arrived at the office. I asked him, "Son, what is wrong between you and me? You have worked hard to not learn." His response was, "Do you know who I am?" I assured him I did, but he asked again, "Do you really know who I am?" I then asked, "Tell me who you are."

"My mother is a prostitute. I'm a bastard!" was his reply. "I don't have a daddy, I've never had a daddy, I have a nickname that means I don't have a daddy. That's who I am, that's all I'll ever be, now you know who I am." His words flowed like a fast running stream. His heart was heavy with pain. I responded to his overflow of feelings with, "Broderick, you are loved by God as if you are God's only child." However, I might as well have been speaking Greek or Hebrew to him for he could not understand a God of steadfast love.

Weeks went by and Broderick took his nineteen years of frustration out on two young men who were all that you would want your son to be—Christian leaders, excellent in academics, good athletes, great relational skills, and campus leaders. These two seemed to understand Broderick, his frustrations, hurts, and disappointments with what life had given him. They would respond to Broderick's actions with, "Broderick, as mean as you are God loves you and we love you." Words that were different from what he had ever heard. One day late in the semester when I entered my office Broderick was waiting. The first words out of his mouth were, "Mrs. Laycock, today I've got the same Daddy you have and I'm somebody." During the night the two students Broderick had aggravated for many weeks had been able to show him the road to his Heavenly Father; he was now "home" with the One who had loved him all his life.

This relationship was possible because God's nature is steadfast love and compassion. But there is another side; God also requires that persons be obedient and Broderick met this criteria. The abiding covenant between God and Broderick continues today as Broderick serves God as a minister in The United Methodist Church. Psalm 103 describes such a relationship in these words: "But the steadfast love of the LORD is from everlasting to everlasting on those who fear him, and his righteousness to children's children, to those who keep his covenant and remember to do his commandments" (vv. 17-18).

The concluding verses of Psalm 103 recall the opening verses of the psalm that proclaim God's reign. It is a glorious description of our relationship with God and God's Creation. When one is in right relationship with God, he or she becomes linked with the whole cosmic order of praise. As a friend says, "Our praise joins the praise of others and the music encircles the earth." May our praise be added to the music of the universe!

Resting Place

REFLECTIONS FOR JOURNALING

Write in your journal: "Bless the LORD, O my soul, and all that is within me, bless his holy name. Bless the LORD, O my soul, and do not forget all his benefits."

- Reflect on and then list the benefits you have received from God. This list can be added to daily.
- Read three psalms each morning for a month as part of your prayer time. They are Psalm 103, a psalm of praise; Psalm 51, asking God to forgive sins and put a right spirit within; and Psalm 91, God's promises of protection.

PRAYER

Thank you, Lord, for your innumerable benefits to me. "Just as I am, thou wilt receive, wilt welcome, pardon, cleanse, relieve; because thy promise I believe, O Lamb of God, I come, I come." Amen. [13]

Psalm 103

Bless the LORD, O my soul,
    and all that is within me,
    bless his holy name.
Bless the LORD, O my soul,
    and do not forget all his benefits—
who forgives all your iniquity,
    who heals all your diseases,
who redeems your life from the Pit,
    who crowns you with steadfast love and mercy,
who satisfies you with good as long as you live
    so that your youth is renewed like the eagle's.
The LORD works vindication and justice for all who
    are oppressed.
He made known his ways to Moses,
    his acts to the people of Israel.
The LORD is merciful and gracious,
    slow to anger and abounding in steadfast love.
He will not always accuse,
    nor will he keep his anger forever.
He does not deal with us according to our iniquities.
For as the heavens are high above the earth,
    so great is his steadfast love
    toward those who fear him;
as far as the east is from the west,
    so far he removes our transgressions from us.
As a father has compassion for his children,
    so the LORD has compassion for those who fear him.
For he knows how we were made;
    he remembers that we are dust.
As for mortals, their days are like grass;
    they flourish like a flower of the field;
for the wind passes over it, and it is gone,
    and its place knows it no more.
But the steadfast love of the LORD is from everlasting
    to everlasting on those who fear him,
    and his righteousness to children's children,
to those who keep his covenant
    and remember to do his commandments.
The LORD has established his throne in the heavens,
    and his kingdom rules over all.
Bless the LORD, O you his angels,
    you mighty ones who do his bidding,
    obedient to his spoken word.
Bless the LORD, all his hosts,
    his ministers that do his will.
Bless the LORD, all his works,
    in all places of his dominion.
Bless the LORD, O my soul.

Praise, My Soul, the King of Heaven

Henry F. Lyte, 1834

1. Praise, my soul, the King of heaven,
    to the throne thy tribute bring;
    ransomed, healed, restored, forgiven,
    evermore God's praises sing.
    Alleluia! Alleluia!
    Praise the everlasting King.

2. Praise, the Lord for grace and favor
    to all people in distress;
    praise God, still the same as ever,
    slow to chide, and swift to bless.
    Alleluia! Alleluia!
    Glorious now God's faithfulness.

3. Fatherlike, God tends and spares us;
    well our feeble frame God knows;
    motherlike, God gently bears us,
    rescues us from all our foes.
    Alleluia! Alleluia!
    Widely yet God's mercy flows.

4. Angels in the heights, adoring,
    you behold God face to face;
    saints triumphant, now adoring,
    gathered in from every race.
    Alleluia! Alleluia!
    Praise with us the God of grace.

Chapter 7

The Palm Sunday Journey

Blessed is the one who comes in the name of the LORD.
Psalm 118:26

The foundation scripture often used for the Palm Sunday message is Luke 19:28-38, Jesus' triumphal entry into Jerusalem. It is a familiar story to many. Jesus sent two disciples to the village of Bethphage with instructions that they would find tied there a colt that had never been ridden. They were to untie it and bring it to Jesus. If the owner of the colt asked why they were taking it, the reply was to be "The Lord needs it."

The disciples did what Jesus told them to do, bringing the colt back with them. They put their cloaks on the donkey's back and lifted Jesus onto the donkey for the ride into Jerusalem. The symbolism in this act is deep, full of hope and joyous expectations. Centuries before Jesus sat on that colt, a prophet named Zechariah had prophesied the following about the Messiah:

Rejoice greatly, O daughter Zion!
  Shout aloud, O daughter Jerusalem!
Lo, your king comes to you;
  triumphant and victorious is he,
humble and riding on a donkey,
  on a colt, the foal of a donkey.
He will cut off the chariot from Ephraim
  and the war-horse from Jerusalem;
and the battle bow shall be cut off,
  and he shall command peace to the nations;
his dominion shall be from sea to sea
  and from the River to the ends of the earth.
(Zech. 9:9-10)

The people who lined the streets on what we now call Palm Sunday knew the Scriptures by memory; now they saw it fulfilled in front of their eyes.

In the ancient world the animal ridden was a clear indicator of the intent of the rider. If a person or an army were on a mission of conquest, a horse was ridden. If coming in peace, a donkey was chosen. Jesus' ride on this day was much more significant than just a two-mile journey on a donkey. It was the culmination and the visible expression of three years of teaching God's truth, engaging people at their point of need, challenging the religious status quo, and living the road to peace. On this day the fulfillment of the words the angels spoke at Jesus' birth were in evidence, "Glory to God in the highest heaven, and on earth peace, goodwill among people" (Luke 2:14).

Many of the people recognized that indeed Jesus was the long-awaited One about whom Zechariah spoke. As Jesus traveled the narrow road (path) down the Mount of Olives, a multitude of disciples began to praise God joyfully for all the deeds of power they had seen (see Luke 19:36-38a). What did they use for this great celebration? Words from the hymnbook of the Temple: "Blessed is the one who comes in the name of the LORD!" (Ps. 118:26a).

Resting Place

REFLECTIONS

Hold in your mind the great joy the people felt as Jesus rode the donkey down the road to Jerusalem. Why do you think the following week they cried, "Crucify him"?

PRAYER

Dear God, as we look at this day now called Palm Sunday, we want to add our songs of praise to the unending circle of Hallel. We praise you, God! Amen.

Psalm 118 is a part of the Hallel collection, which is composed of Psalms 113–118. The Hebrew word *hallel* means "praise" and this collection was and is used at all major festivals, especially at the beginning and end of Passover.[14] Just as Psalm 118 had been used to praise God for the saving events of the Exodus and the return from the exile, on Palm Sunday, voices were again raised in song to praise God for the gift of Jesus, the long-awaited Messiah. This was a definite sign of God's continuing presence and ongoing help for humankind. Hallelujah!

As we reflect on this psalm, important questions begin to surface. For example, what are visible signs in the world arena of

God's continuing presence and care? Where do we see persons riding a donkey (being peacemakers) into places plagued with war, devastation, crime, poverty, hopelessness, and injustice? Where can we sing a *Hallel* song?

I wish it were possible to take you to Ibillin, Galilee, a Palestinian village seventeen miles north of Nazareth. Here you would meet a Palestinian Melkite priest, Father Elias Chacour. As a young boy Father Chacour saw his village destroyed. He shares the story in these words:

> In 1948, Zionist soldiers had tricked the people of Biram into leaving by telling them about an imaginary attack and giving worthless written guarantee of return. After two weeks in the nearby fields, we discovered our warm, pleasant village life in Biram was gone forever. The soldiers had ransacked our houses and ruined our food supply. Most of the village men were herded into trucks at gunpoint and driven away. Old people, women and children were left to fend for themselves.[15]

Instead of becoming bitter, resentful, and bursting with anger, Father Chacour continued his education and was ordained into the priesthood. His assignment was to a church in Ibillin where the former priest had stripped the church of all its furnishings except the old benches and stone altar. Father Chacour was not well received by parishioners. As a matter of fact he was blatantly told, "We don't want you here!" However, his call was from God, not people; he knew he was to serve the church and build a school for the children. Neither of these came easily. The complete story can be found in Chacour's book *We Belong to the Land*.

I do want to share with you what is currently taking place in the schools, which were built in spite of great mental, physical, and spiritual persecution. These schools, the Mar Elias Educational Institutions, are the road to peace in Israel. The current enrollment (April 1, 2002) is shown here.[16]

Kindergarten	245
Elementary School	145
High School	1,550
Technical College	750
Regional Teachers Center	1,200
School for Gifted Children	160
Total	4,050

You may wonder why I am so excited about this educational system. If you look at the background of the students you will understand. The makeup of the student body is most unique: Jews, Palestinian Muslims, Druze and Palestinian Christians—children from the major religions of Israel are going to school together. The faculty is also made up of the same mix. These persons learn to live together in mutual respect. They will not always agree but through studying, playing, eating, singing, and working together they experience justice and equality—pathways to peace. Here are the potential peacemakers for Israel!

Father Chacour, in choosing to follow the example of Jesus, is the living presence of Christ's spirit. The purpose of this journey is to bring justice, mercy, and love to all persons.

Blessed are they who come in the name of the Lord!

Resting Place

REFLECTIONS
- Can you think of an example of dividing walls being torn down between persons?
- Ask God to show you how to be a peacemaker in the areas of life in which you live.

PRAYER
O God, show me how to walk in the way of peace and justice. "Breathe on me, Breath of God, fill me with life anew, that I may love what thou dost love, and do what thou wouldst do."[17]

༺❀༻

Blessed are they who come in the name of the Lord!

The horrific conflict currently going on in Israel between the Jews and the Palestinians has cost the lives of many on both sides. It is similar to the story about Father Chacour but it, too, illustrates how even wounds that are rooted in centuries of hate can be put aside and individuals can collectively come together as peacemakers. The story appeared in *USA Today*. It was written by an Israeli and a Palestinian who lost close relations during the current intifada, which began in September 2000. Ghazi Brigit and Yitzhak Frankenthal wrote:

We have every reason to despise each other, to be mortal enemies. One of us is an Israeli whose son was kidnapped and killed five
years ago by Hamas. The other is a Palestinian whose brother was
killed by Israeli troops at a checkpoint in his village. But our grief
unites us behind the same goal.

As part of a delegation representing 350 Palestinian and Israeli
families whose loved ones were killed in the blood feud between our
peoples, we are coming to the United States next week to plead with
the Bush administration, the United Nations and the European Union
to stop the insane violence that our leaders are unable—or unwill-
ing—to prevent.

Many parents who have lost sons and daughters in this conflict
are angry and demand revenge. We are no less angry with those who
took our loved ones away, but we demand peace and reconciliation.

We are not diplomats, politicians or "experts" on the Middle East
with Ph.D.s. We are experts on the price paid by the relatives of more
than 1,400 Palestinians and Israelis killed in this conflict since the
intifada began in September 2000. But we understand that our leaders are offering no solutions, no paths out of the darkness and back to
the negotiating tables.[18]

This group came in the name of peace. In their article there is one
sentence that keeps surfacing in my heart: "But our grief unites us
behind the same goal." It brings to mind the words of Jesus: "If you,
even you, had only recognized on this day the things that make for
peace! But now they are hidden from your eyes" (Luke 19:42).

I am firmly convinced that the more we love, the more we
grieve. I also believe the more we love the more joy we experience.
These experiences usually go hand in hand as we participate in the
universal heartbeat of persons and groups. Peace can never be
achieved with a "Band-Aid approach"—covering over the problem
and leaving the root intact. Peace is present when we can truly say
to all, "You are my brother, you are my sister! And I will work for
your highest good." The Palestinian and Israeli delegates who
came to America risked being misunderstood or ostracized for
supporting a cause that is unpopular in many circles, and they
came at great personal expense both in time and money. However,
their shared pain was the common ground that moved them as one
to seek the road to peace. May many voices sing a *Hallel* song for
their courage and commitment.

Blessed are they who come in the name of the Lord!

Resting Place

REFLECTIONS FOR JOURNALING
- Name a recent experience of riding a donkey (being a peace-maker) in a specific situation.
- Write about a recent experience in which you sang a *Hallel* (praise) song about the continuing presence and ongoing help received from God.
- Write from your own experience how the more you love, the more you grieve. Have you also known more joy?

PRAYER
Help us, O God, to love so deeply that we move into the pain of the world and serve as peacemakers. Amen.

Psalm 118

O give thanks to the LORD, for he is good;
    his steadfast love endures forever!
Let Israel say,
    "His steadfast love endures forever."
Let the house of Aaron say,
    "His steadfast love endures forever."
Let those who fear the LORD say,
    "His steadfast love endures forever."
Out of my distress I called on the LORD;
    the LORD answered me and set me in a broad place.
With the LORD on my side I do not fear.
    What can mortals do to me?
The LORD is on my side to help me;
    I shall look in triumph on those who hate me.
It is better to take refuge in the LORD
    than to put confidence in mortals.
It is better to take refuge in the LORD
    than to put confidence in princes.
All nations surrounded me;
    in the name of the LORD I cut them off!
They surrounded me,
    surrounded me on every side;
    in the name of the LORD I cut them off!
They surrounded me like bees;
    they blazed like a fire of thorns;
    in the name of the LORD I cut them off!
I was pushed hard, so that I was falling,
    but the LORD helped me.
The LORD is my strength and my might;

he has become my salvation.
There are glad songs of victory in the tents of the righteous:
"The right hand of the LORD does valiantly;
  the right hand of the LORD is exalted;
  the right hand of the LORD does valiantly."
I shall not die, but I shall live.
  and recount the deeds of the LORD.
The LORD has punished me severely,
  but he did not give me over to death.
Open to me the gates of righteousness,
  that I may enter through them
  and give thanks to the LORD.
This is the gate of the LORD;
  the righteous shall enter through it.
I thank you that you have answered me
  and have become my salvation.
The stone that the builders rejected
  has become the chief cornerstone.
This is the LORD's doing;
  it is marvelous in our eyes.
This is the day that the LORD has made;
  let us rejoice and be glad in it.
Save us, we beseech you, O LORD!
  O LORD, we beseech you, give us success!
Blessed is the one who comes in the name of the LORD.
  We bless you from the house of the LORD.
The LORD is God,
  and he has given us light.
Bind the festal procession with branches,
  up to the horns of the altar.
You are my God, and I will give thanks to you;
  you are my God, I will extol you.
O give thanks to the LORD, for he is good,
  for his steadfast love endures forever.

This Is the Day the Lord Hath Made

Isaac Watts, 1719

This is the day the Lord hath made;
  he calls the hours his own.
Let heaven rejoice, let earth be glad,
  and praise surround the throne.

Chapter 8

Psalms from the Cross

"My God, my God, why have you forsaken me?"
Psalm 22:1a

In the closing moments of Jesus' life, two of his prayers to God were from the book of Psalms. As we forget our twenty-first-century world and listen to these prayers through first-century Middle Eastern ears, we gain a new understanding of what these words meant to the diverse crowd of persons gathered together on the Golgotha hillside on this dark Friday.

There were persons at the foot of the cross, and persons today, who believe that God is too pure to look upon the kind of suffering Jesus experienced on the cross. At that horrific event, God turned away from Jesus. When that happened Jesus cried out, "My God, my God, why have you forsaken me?" Such a viewpoint, in my mind, is totally foreign to God's nature. In fact, we are taught by Jesus, "Those who love me will keep my word, and my Father will love them, and we will come to them and make our home with them" (John 14:23). This promise does not portray a God who forsakes, but one who abides in all circumstances.

To further substantiate the ever-present God, in Psalm 56 we hear the psalmist say he has had a rough night, but he knows that God is with him. "You have kept count of my tossings; put my tears in your bottle. Are they not in your record?" (v. 8). This is a reference to a Middle Eastern custom that is many centuries old. When persons cried either for joy or for sorrow, they held a little tear bottle under each eye and collected their tears. Persons had one pair of tear bottles for tears of joy, and one pair for tears of sorrow. After collecting the tears, they were poured out in a meaningful way. An example of such action is found in the story of the woman coming into the house of Simon the Pharisee when Jesus is present. Her entrance into this house was strictly forbidden by Jewish law, but in a faith crisis one does not think about law, but about survival. Luke records this meeting in these words, "And a woman in the city, who was a sinner, having heard that he [Jesus] was eating in the Pharisee's house, brought an alabaster jar of ointment. She stood behind him at his feet, weeping, and began to bathe his feet with her tears" (Luke 7:37-38a). She may have bathed the feet of Jesus by pouring out her tears from a pair of tear bottles.

When the psalmist asks God to "put my tears in your bottle. Are they not in your record?" he is expressing faith in the living God who also cries, cares, hurts, and records the concerns of people—not in a God who abandons in a time of crisis.

Why, then, did Jesus cry, "My God, my God, why have you forsaken me?"

Resting Place

REFLECTIONS
Read Psalm 22.
- Can you identify similarities between what the psalmist has experienced and what Jesus experienced during the final hours of his life?

PRAYER
Dearest Jesus, I come to your cross of sorrow, knowing that you count my tears and understand my own grief. "Near the cross! O Lamb of God, bring its scenes before me; help me walk from day to day with its shadow o'er me." Amen. [19]

In studying Psalm 22 many similarities can be found between the life of the psalmist and Jesus' experience on that fateful Friday:

- I am scorned by others.
- I am despised by the people.
- All who see me mock at me.
- They make mouths at me.
- They shake their heads.
- I am poured out like water, and all my bones are out of joint.
- My heart is like wax, it is melted within my breast.
- My mouth is dried up like a potsherd.
- My tongue sticks to my jaws.
- They stare and gloat over me.
- They divide my clothes among themselves, and for my clothing they cast lots.

Aren't there striking similarities between the treatment given the psalmist and what the crowd at the foot of the cross did to Jesus?

We are now back to the question: Why did Jesus quote Psalm 22:1? Look at the closing words of the psalm:

> To him, indeed, shall all who sleep in the earth bow down;
>   before him shall bow all who go down to the dust,
>   and I shall live for him.
> Posterity will serve him;
>   future generations will be told about the Lord,
> and proclaim his deliverance to a people yet unborn,
>   saying that he has done it. (vv. 29-31)

These are not words of desperation, but a visualization of what the future will be; what God intends for the world. God will reign over all peoples and nations in all times, places, and circumstances—even though at the present time that appears to the contrary. Therefore, Jesus' cry from the cross using Psalm 22:1 is an affirmation of faith in God. The Crucifixion will (1) serve posterity as an atonement for sin; (2) serve future generations in revealing the self-giving love of Jesus and God; and (3) show how God shares in all human affliction.

Resting Place

REFLECTIONS
- In the midst of pain, sorrow, misfortune, and /or rejection, can you affirm that this, too, will be used to serve in God's plan for righteousness?
- Reflect on the promise that "all things work together for good for those who love God" (Rom. 8:28).

PRAYER
O God, thank you for Jesus' willingness to suffer on the cross so that I can know your love and mercy. "In the cross of Christ I glory, towering o'er the wrecks of time; all the light of sacred story gathers round its head sublime." Amen. [20]

Another meaningful insight into this psalm was gained while teaching in Israel. I talked with my friend Father Elias Chacour about a theory I had regarding what could have happened at the foot of the cross when Jesus began to cry, "My God, my God, why have you forsaken me?"

In the first century CE few people could read and write. The majority of people never read the holy writings; they depended on the priests and scribes to read for them. However, the populace had become very adept in memorization—they knew many scriptures by heart. Therefore, it is possible that when Jesus began quoting from the psalm, those at the foot of the cross who were of the Jewish faith could quote the psalm from beginning to end. In using this opening verse Jesus was inviting his friends and loved ones to see from the holy writings that the horrendous suffering he was experiencing would be used by God to serve future generations. He did not want the suffering, but he embraced it for others. He faced death with the confident assurance that the power of God was greater than the power of death. And he knew that God shared in his suffering.

In quoting from Psalm 22, Jesus gave a message of comfort to those who were devastated; he reminded them that suffering can bring glory to God, and that God's future would be served by the Crucifixion. The day of the Crucifixion was a dark Friday, but it was followed by a glorious Easter Sunday!

Father Chacour confirmed the idea that those at the foot of the cross would have known the psalm by heart and could have quoted it word for word. The art of memorization was and is an important characteristic of Middle Eastern culture. It is also known to some extent in twenty-first-century American culture. Most people who hear "The Lord is my shepherd," are able to repeat the remainder of the psalm.

Resting Place

REFLECTIONS
* Reflect on an event in your life when you felt abandonment. Did you invite God into this dark night/day of the soul? Did this experience produce any deeper roots in God? If so, can you name these roots?

PRAYER

O God of the ages, help me to see beyond what is to what can be. May I never forget your greatness: "Great are the works of the LORD, studied by all who delight in them" Amen. (Ps. 111:2)

⟡

"Into your hands I commit my spirit."
On the cross Jesus prayed a second prayer from the book of Psalms. The Gospel of Luke records, "Then Jesus, crying with a loud voice, said, 'Father, into your hands I commend my spirit.' Having said this, he breathed his last" (Luke 23:46). This prayer comes from Psalm 31:5 and through the centuries has provided a very special relationship with God for our Jewish sisters and brothers, even to this moment.

Jesus' final words from the cross were voiced with this prayer; but these words are not simply an interpretation of how Jesus died, but also of how he lived. In the Jewish tradition, when a baby was born into a family it was the duty of the father or mother to pray over the child each evening at bedtime. The prescribed prayer was "Into your hand I commit my spirit." When the child had language, these were the words he or she was to pray just before going to sleep. It is a prayer that entrusts both our present and future to God.

A close reading of the prayer of Jesus will reveal the addition of one word: "Father." One of Jesus' favorite names for God was Father. In the Lord's Prayer we are taught to pray "Our Father." In John's Gospel Jesus says, "My Father is still working, and I also am working" (John 5:17). Jesus also promises his followers: "Everything that the Father gives me will come to me, and anyone who comes to me I will never drive away" (John 6:37). It is not at all surprising that one of the last words of Jesus was the word "Father."

The Aramaic word for father is *Abba*. It has a unique and gracious meaning in the Middle East even today. The parable of the prodigal son is now called "the Father" or "the waiting Father." It is Jesus' attempt to show the nature of God as Father (see Luke 15:11-32). This pearl of the parables teaches that God, who is Abba, is one who:
• gives steadfast and unconditional love
• meets each child where he or she is and seeks an abiding relationship
• is faithful in every way
• enters into the pain, sorrow, joy, and dreams of the child

- extends forgiveness and restores the relationship as a full member of the family
- welcomes and celebrates the return home of a child
- never stops seeking to be in right relationships with the son or daughter

This beautiful understanding of the nature of God is why Jesus adds the word "Father" to the traditional prayer. Jesus' final act of his earthly life is an affirmation of trust in God who is his Abba. Following the example of Jesus, several of the saints of the church are said to have died with the words of Psalm 31:5 on their lips, including Jerome, Martin Luther, and John Knox.[21]

Resting Place

REFLECTIONS
- Jesus taught us how to fully live, trusting God day and night. Is this possible?
- When you lie down to sleep, pray this prayer with total confidence that God takes the night shift.
- In the morning, pray the same prayer for the day.

PRAYER
Father, into your hand I commit my spirit. Amen.

What does it mean for us to turn our lives and our future over to God? It is very difficult to give up management of our lives and totally surrender all to the leadership of God. Many have heard the inspiring story of two young women, Dayna Curry and Heather Mercer, who were serving as foreign aid workers in the poverty-stricken land of Kabul, Afghanistan. On August 3, 2001 the two women were arrested. Even now, Curry and Mercer say they are not sure why they were actually arrested. The serious charge of prose-lytizing was placed against them but both women say they were 100 percent innocent of that charge. The activity of proselytizing is defined by the Taliban as seeking Christian conversions in exchange for humanitarian aid. Curry and Mercer said that talking to Afghan people about matters of faith was a normal activity in which they shared as they served the people. The Afghans would share about Allah and how Allah was their one God, and often they would ask the foreign aid workers about their faith. No proselytizing was practiced. Speaking at their alma mater, Baylor University in Waco, Texas, about their six-week imprisonment in Afghanistan, I think we can hear how they would answer the question: "What does it mean to turn our lives and our futures over to God?"

> "As the days went on and the interrogation started," Mercer said, "I became extremely afraid. For a month and a half, that fear escalated. I feared that the religious police were going to execute us; I feared that we'd spend our whole lives in prison; I feared that a terrorist group would know where we were and kill us; and, eventually, I feared that we would lose our lives from a bomb. I was immobilized at times—physically just shaking with fear."
>
> "Finally," Mercer said, she came to a turning point. "I remember the scripture that said, 'If you lose your life, you'll find it. But if you save your life, you'll lose it.' I was so afraid to die that I was just trying to save my own life. And I'd lost it. I didn't have joy. I didn't have control. When I finally said, 'If I die, I die for Jesus. And, if I live, I live for him,' there was so much freedom."[22]

In these words I again hear the prayer of Jesus on the cross, "Father, into you hands I commit my spirit." To belong to God in living and dying means ultimately that we bring to God our whole being for servanthood ministry, knowing that "God's faithfulness and love enable and empower the existence of a people who in turn can be faithful and loving to God and to each other."[23] In our world full of isolated selves coping with terror all around, this is Good News!

Resting Place

REFLECTIONS FOR JOURNALING
Let us have the courage to ask the question:
• What does it mean for me to pray, "Father, into your hands I commit my spirit"? God is eager to answer this cry of our hearts.

PRAYER
God, I bring as much of myself as I understand to as much of you as I understand. Tomorrow I will bring more because I have been with you all day today. Amen.

Psalm 22

My God, my God, why have you forsaken me?
Why are you so far from helping me, from the words
    of my groaning?
O my God, I cry by day, but you do not answer;
    and by night, but find no rest.
Yet you are holy,
    enthroned on the praises of Israel.
In you our ancestors trusted;
    they trusted, and you delivered them.
To you they cried, and were saved;
    in you they trusted, and were not put to shame.
But I am a worm, and not human;
    scorned by others, and despised by the people.
All who see me mock at me:
    they make mouths at me, they shake their heads;
"Commit your cause to the LORD;
    let him deliver—
    let him rescue the one in whom he delights!"
Yet it was you who took me from the womb;
    you kept me safe on my mother's breast,
On you I was cast from my birth,
    and since my mother bore me you have been my God.
Do not be far from me,
    for trouble is near
    and there is no one to help.
Many bulls encircle me,
    strong bulls of Bashan surround me;
they open wide their mouths at me,
    like a ravening and roaring lion.
I am poured out like water,
    and all my bones are out of joint;
my heart is like wax;
    it is melted within my breast;
my mouth is dried up like a potsherd,
    and my tongue sticks to my jaws;
    you lay me in the dust of death.
For dogs are all around me;
    a company of evildoers encircle me.
My hands and feet have shriveled;
    I can count all my bones.
They stare and gloat over me;
    they divide my clothes among themselves,
    and for my clothing they cast lots.
But you, O LORD, do not be far away!
    O my help, come quickly to my aid!
Deliver my soul from the sword,
    my life from the power of the dog!
Save me from the mouth of the lion!
    From the horns of the wild oxen you have rescued me.
I will tell of your name to my brothers and sisters;
    in the midst of the congregation I will praise you:
You who fear the LORD, praise him!

All you offspring of Jacob, glorify him;
    stand in awe of him, all you offspring of Israel!
For he did not despise or abhor
    the affliction of the afflicted;
he did not hide his face from me,
    but heard when I cried to him.
From you comes my praise in the great congregation;
    my vows I will pay before those who fear him.
The poor shall eat and be satisfied;
    those who seek him shall praise the LORD.
    May your hearts live forever!
All the ends of the earth shall remember
    and turn to the LORD;
    and all the families of the nations
    shall worship before him.
For dominion belongs to the LORD,
    and he rules over the nations.
To him, indeed, shall all who sleep in the earth bow down;
    before him shall bow all who go down to the dust,
    and I shall live for him.
Posterity will serve him;
    future generations will be told about the LORD,
and proclaim his deliverance to a people yet unborn,
    saying that he has done it.

O Sacred Head, Now Wounded
Anonymous Latin; trans. by Paul Gerhardt, 1656,
and James W. Alexander, 1830

1. O sacred Head, now wounded, with grief and shame weighed down,
now scornfully surrounded with thorns, thine only crown:
how pale thou art with anguish, with sore abuse and scorn!
How does that visage languish which once was bright as morn!

2. What thou, my Lord, hast suffered was all for sinners' gain;
mine, mine was the transgression, but thine the deadly pain.
Lo, here I fall, my Savior! 'Tis I deserve thy place;
look on me with thy favor, vouchsafe to me thy grace.

3. What language shall I borrow to thank thee, dearest friend,
for this thy dying sorrow, thy pity without end?
O make me thine forever; and should I fainting be,
Lord, let me never, never outlive my love to thee.

Chapter 9

The Other Bookend

Praise the LORD!
Psalm 150:1*a*

Bring on the full orchestra! Invite all humanity to join the choir! Include everything that breathes in the celebration! Give praise to God! Do not forget the instruments!

With great fanfare Psalm 150 invites all of God's creatures to yield themselves in praise to God. The reason for praise is God's surpassing greatness to all. God is Creator, God is sovereign, God is steadfast love, God is our guide, God gives grace, God forgives—the list is endless. What better way to say thanks to God than through praise music?

Music is God's gift, one that transcends all barriers separating people from one another and humans from other creatures. To participate in music is to be close to the heart of God. Psalm 150 enthusiastically invites all to sing praises to God in the sanctuary and to praise God throughout the universe. In worship, work, and play—make life a continuous, joyful song of praise. This song needs the melodious accompaniment of musical instruments, so use them all without restraint. The God of all life needs to be praised with the great sounds that generate from life.

Years ago there was a song titled "I'd Like to Teach the World to Sing." It carried a simple, but profound message about world harmony. This same theme is found in Psalm 150. The whole world, humanity and nature, has the capacity for music. As we add our note to the music there will be a world of harmony, beauty, and pleasing sounds. Psalm 150 joyfully calls us all to become a symphony of praise to God.

Psalm 1 and Psalm 150 are indeed "bookends," for they are the first and last psalms of the collection. Psalm 150 is certainly fitting for this placement. Praise is the offering of one's whole life and self to God. Psalm 150 invites us to full participation in life. For that reason Psalm 150 serves not only as a bookend, but also as an appropriate doxology to the reader and to the book of Psalms. May we accept the invitation to be a part of the music of the universe.

REFLECTIONS
- Praise of God has been expressed through the centuries in many hearts and languages.
- Write your own song of praise to add to this vast repertoire.

PRAYER

O God, I want to add my song of praise to that heard throughout the world. "The church with psalms must shout, no door can keep them out. But, more than all, my heart must bear the longest part. Let all the world in every corner sing: my God and King!" Amen. [24]

Psalm 150

Praise the LORD!
Praise God in his sanctuary;
   praise him in his mighty firmament!
Praise him for his mighty deeds;
   praise him according to his surpassing greatness!
Praise him with trumpet sound;
   praise him with lute and harp!
Praise him with tambourine and dance;
   praise him with strings and pipe!
Praise him with clanging cymbals;
   praise him with loud crashing cymbals!
Let everything that breathes praise the LORD!
Praise the LORD!

Praise to the Lord, the Almighty

Joachim Neander, 1680

1. Praise to the Lord, the Almighty, the King of creation!
   O my soul, praise him, for he is thy health and salvation!
   All ye who hear, now to his temple draw near;
   join me in glad adoration!

2. Praise to the Lord, who doth prosper thy work and defend thee;
   surely his goodness and mercy here daily attend thee.
   Ponder anew what the Almighty can do,
   who with his love doth befriend thee.

3. Praise to the Lord! O let all that is in me adore him!
   All that hath life and breath, come now with praises
        before him!
   Let the amen sound from his people again;
   gladly forever adore him.

Notes

1. "I Want Jesus to Walk with Me" in *The United Methodist Hymnal* (Nashville: The United Methodist Publishing House, 1989), no. 521.

2. Eugenia Price, *Maria* (New York: Bantam Books, Harper & Row, 1977), p. 414.

3. Nathaniel Hawthorne, *The Complete Short Stories of Nathaniel Hawthorne* (Garden City, N.Y.: Doubleday, 1959), p. 473.

4. *The New Interpreter's Bible*, volume IV (Nashville: Abingdon Press, 1996), pp. 710-11.

5. Data collected from author's studies of physics.

6. Saint Augustine of Hippo, *Confessions*, book 1, chapter 1.

7. *New Interpreter's Bible*, Vol. IV, p. 711.

8. Ibid., p. 769.

9. Gloria Gaither and William Gaither, "Because He Lives" in *The United Methodist Hymnal* (Nashville: The United Methodist Publishing House, 1989), no. 364.

10. Maxie Dunnam, *This Is Christianity* (Nashville: Abingdon Press, 1994), p. 28.

11. *New Interpreter's Bible*, vol. IV, p. 1091.

12. The Jesus Doll™ was created to be a visual reminder of Jesus' constant presence with adults and children at all levels of faith. For more information, contact IN STITCHES: Center for Liturgical Art, 17092 Sunset Dr., Chagrin Falls, OH 44023; 1-888-683-7074; www.institchescenter.com/jesusdoll.

13. Charlotte Elliott, "Just as I Am, Without One Plea" in *The United Methodist Hymnal*, (Nashville: The United Methodist Publishing House, 1989), no. 357, stanza 5.

14. *New Interpreter's Bible*, vol. IV, p. 1138.

15. Elias Chacour, *We Belong to the Land* (San Francisco: Harper, 1990), p. 6.

16. From "The Pilgrims' Post," vol. 6, Winter 2002, p. 3.

17. Edwin Hatch, "Breathe on Me, Breath of God" in *The United Methodist Hymnal* (Nashville: The United Methodist Publishing House, 1989), no 420, stanza 1.

18. *USA Today*, March 15, 2002, p. 15A.

19. Fanny Crosby, "Jesus, Keep Me Near the Cross" in *The United Methodist Hymnal* (Nashville: The United Methodist Publishing House, 1989), no. 301, stanza 3.

20. John Bowring, "In the Cross of Christ I Glory" in *The United Methodist Hymnal*, no. 295, stanza 1.

21. *New Interpreter's Bible*, vol. IV, p. 802.

22. *The Baylor Line*, Winter 2002, Alumni Magazine, Baylor University, Waco, Texas, pp. 28-29.

23. *New Interpreter's Bible*, vol. IV, p. 803.

24. George Herbert, "Let All the World in Every Corner Sing," *The United Methodist Hymnal*, no. 93, stanza 2.